# The God of
# Second Chances

# The God of
# Second Chances

## STORIES OF LIVES
## TRANSFORMED BY FAITH

## MARCIA Z. NELSON

### FOREWORD BY PHYLLIS TICKLE

SHEED & WARD

Franklin, Wisconsin
Chicago

As an apostolate of the Priests of the Sacred Heart, a Catholic religious congregation, the mission of Sheed & Ward is to publish books of contemporary impact and enduring merit in Catholic Christian thought and action. The books published, however, reflect the opinion of their authors and are not meant to represent the official position of the Priests of the Sacred Heart.

2001

Sheed & Ward
7373 South Lovers Lane Road
Franklin, Wisconsin 53132
1-800-266-5564

Printed in the United States of America

Cover photograph by Mary Heller/The Image Bank. Used with permission.
Cover design: Kathy Kikkert
Interior design: GrafixStudio

Thomas R. Kelly (p. xiii) quotation from *A Testament of Devotion* (HarperSanFrancisco, 1992 [original 1941]). Used by permission.

"Gravy" (p. xxii) from *A New Path to the Waterfall*, Raymond Carver. Copyright © 1989 by the estate of Raymond Carver. Used by permission of Grove/Atlantic, Inc.

Scripture quotations are from the New Revised Standard Version of the Bible, copyright 1946, 1952, 1971 by the Division of Christian Education of the National Council of the Churches of Christ in the USA. Used by permission. All rights reserved.

**Library of Congress Cataloging-in-Publication Data**

Nelson, Marcia Z.
    The God of second chances : stories of lives transformed
by faith / Marcia Z. Nelson;
    Foreword by Phyllis Tickle.
    p. cm.
  ISBN 1-58051-105-8 (pbk.)
    Spiritual biography—United States. 2. Change
(Psychology)—Religious aspects. I. Title.
  BL72 .N445  2001
  291.4'2—dc21                 2001041158

1 2 3 4 5 / 04 03 02 01

For my mother, father, husband, daughter, son

*It takes generations*

# Contents

# Foreword

"Hope springs eternal in the human breast," or so Alexander Pope claimed when, three hundred years ago, he wrote his *An Essay on Man*. Because we like that sentiment, we have always honored Pope's line, repeating it to our children and to each other with such frequency and on so routine a basis that it has become a kind of cultural touchstone or cliché. What we have managed to ignore and indeed, in more recent decades, completely forget, is the rest of the poet's words about our human condition.

The enlightened Mr. Pope was far too much a product of his times and personally of far too cynical a disposition to leave us for long in such a state of ongoing beneficence. What he argues, instead, in the very next and now forgotten lines of his *Essay* is that hope is all hope is, that in fact "Man never is, but always to be blest." Written less metrically and with contemporary stylistic conventions, we would render the line: "Man never *is*, but always [is] *to be* blest." And by that teasing out of Pope's meaning we expose the bitterness that hides just beyond the lovely face of hope. We expose the possibility, ever present in human affairs, that hope just might be its own end and that faith might be its own reward. If so, then to what point life? For what reason existence?

Those are serious questions, ones that, while they may have afflicted Alexander Pope's era at an intellectual level, did not achieve their fullest, most demonic power to ravage human emotion and human purpose until the twentieth century. It was then that we Euro-Americans began first to engage and finally to co-habit with them in the words and principles of existential angst.

The book you are about to read is a very simple one . . . simple in its words, simple in its accessible stories and post-cards, simple in its thesis. As such and in its very ordinariness of tone and tale, *The God of Second Chances* is light-years removed in both weight and form from Pope's cynicism and existentialism's spiritual paralysis. As such, however, it is also a kind of twenty-first-century antidote to them.

By her own admission, Marcia Nelson is a student of hope. In this book she reveals herself also as a tough, well-traveled, sophisticated believer in a God whose mercy is the source and substance of hope. In good, twenty-first-century investigative fashion, Nelson leaves the theoretical preserve of her family, her office, and her work as a professional journalist to explore the question of hope by exploring the actuality of human redemp-tion and change and—yes—of blessing. From the skid-row bleakness of San Francisco's Tenderloin to the elegance of a successful bed & breakfast Delta-style to the quiet steadiness of Philadelphia's Quaker community, we follow Nelson as she elicits and records in their own words stories of human beings who, in desperation, have accepted hope at its face value and then used it as a passage through hell and into love . . . or as St. Paul, that other oft-quoted authority on the subject, would have it, into charity.

In the course of her travels, Nelson sends us postcards as well, postcards that, unlike the stories, tell us about our reporter and not her subjects. In an effective way, those postcards from cities scattered across the country, and from Marcia Nelson's younger, more private life, are also Marcia Nelson's credentials. They are her authority for telling us these stories. Our reporter is, in other words, her own best proof-text; and the fact that we come to know and like her as a human being while we profit from her as a journalist is no small part of the adventure as we go with her on this journey in search of the God of Second Chances.

Phyllis Tickle
Lucy, Tennessee
Pentecost 2001

# Introduction

> *God the Lover, the accuser, the revealer*
> *of Light and darkness presses within us.*
> *"Behold I stand at the door and knock."*
> *And all our apparent initiative is already a*
> *response, a testimonial to his secret presence*
> *and working within us.*

—Thomas R. Kelly, *A Testament of Devotion*

Fortunately for us mistake-prone humans, God allows U-turns.

U-turns are the grace of second chances. This book of stories chronicles many such chances, U-turns or turning points experienced by ordinary men and women who came to realize the power of faith to transform tough circumstances and to redeem mistakes. Circumstances of stumbling or affliction can simultaneously be laboratories for human transformation and the alchemy of adversity. That alchemy requires a common element: faith, an acknowledgment of the secret presence already within.

The traditional process of alchemy has a thoroughly modern equivalent: recycling. One day in 1994, my then-editor Mike Chapin and I were discussing a mutual acquaintance we had just shared lunch with. Reverend Paul Johannaber, a longtime local clergy leader, was getting on in years, we observed, and had certainly earned the right to slow down. We both agreed that the man behind the local mission for drunks and addicts, having served as county-jail chaplain for fifty years, had turned a lot of earthly dross to gold.

As an editor would, Mike turned a wonderful phrase while the car idled at a red light.

"Paul," he said, "recycles people."

This proved to be a memorable description of the process of deep transformation, of the transmutation that liberates what is best out of the worst and most abject. Like little seeds, his words entered my imagination and began to grow over time.

This book is the result. Inside this book—a chronicle of surprises and openness—is a small helping of hope. These are stories of lives utterly transformed by faith. They record the rebirth of hope in the lives of ordinary people. Like Sarah's Isaac, hope is the unlikely child, born late in life's experience.

Over and over again in researching and writing this book, I heard the same longing expressed in many different settings: people are hungry for hope. Anecdotes, headlines, and surveys document this hunger even in the midst of the land of plenty: plenty of stimulation, plenty of diversion, plenty of accessories for the good life.

The hope yielded through faith's transformation is not false hope, short-lived and ill equipped to ride out a rough journey. It's not cheap hope; those living a new life have paid with the hard currency of mistakes that took years of their lives. It's not easy hope; coming to God can be a journey of heel-dragging, kicking, and screaming profanities, like a drunk seizure-ing his way into sobriety, aching for a drink of the water of life. On the very road to hell, God sets up detours to a new place.

This book is also the result of a career-long passion for and fascination with stories of those who have been hell-bent for hell but given, through grace, an opportunity to change their direction and their ways. As a writer I have been drawn to the tales of people who, troubled in soul and mind, have been addicts, gangbangers, and hell-raisers but, like Lazarus, were given another chance and raised to new life, a transformed life with opportunities to do good and reach others in similar circumstances, using their lives as teaching text.

U-turns are one dramatic, difficult, and known path to sainthood, a path of irony and providence. The persecutor Saul became the Christian advocate Paul. The Tibetan Buddhist holy man Milarepa began his days as a murderous sorcerer and ended them as an enlightened being. Moses spent his earliest years among the oppressors of his people. But not everyone who has embraced faith passionately has had to repent of wrongdoing. Rather, some were accosted on everyday roads, shaken out of quiet existence and ordinary expectations by the rude wake-up of trauma, serious illness, accident, or loss—all of them catastrophes that close one path and force a change of direction.

The journey of change proceeds along a road of new possibilities. Call the process *transformation, resurrection, rehabilitation, survival, recovery.* As represented by each of the people in this book, this process has many faces, many names: the recovering alcoholic or junkie, the rehabilitated felon, the forgiving victim, the illness survivor. These make good stories, providing a window on what is best about us and also most human: the ability to make mistakes, make amends, and make good. As stories, they are inspiring; as examples, they offer living proof of what so many despair of: that change will overhaul the human heart and any, or all, of us can live better lives.

These stories are common, although often untold. By radar and research, I deliberately set out to find them, searching for stories that differed in specifics but shared a pattern of radical, faith-powered transformation. I looked for people from various walks of life. I looked in different cities that would represent different corners on the map. I looked in cities where I had been and in places new to me. From Chicago to San Francisco to New Orleans, I found business people, people in the helping professions, performers, ministers, volunteers. They represented different points on the religious spectrum, a sampling neither exhaustive nor comprehensive but nonetheless diverse: Catholic Christian, Jewish, a variety of Protestant Christians, and one or two whose unconventional expressions of faith defied conventional labels. Looking around the country for people to write about at first seemed impossibly ambitious and inevitably arbitrary. Yet it gave me momentum, and it also deepened my conviction that the transformation process I was writing about was a common one, not confined to race, region, religion, class, or gender.

Reflecting this diversity, the spiritual power energizing the transformation that each of the people in this book experienced, and continue to experience, answers to many different names. Some call this power Jesus Christ—and the evangelical Christians I have profiled prefer this language. Paul writes excitedly in his second letter to the Corinthians: "So if anyone is in Christ, there is a new creation: everything old has passed away; see, everything has become new!" (2 Corinthians 5:17) Others believe God has many names, and use different terms: Higher Power, God, Allah, Sophia, Divinity, the Center, the Inner Light. I have tried to approach the name, and the understanding, of God as ecumenically and eclectically as possible. For one thing, it obviates hundreds of years of theological tussling to believe that God has given us many roads. A narrow road to heaven would make for one big traffic jam, inciting a lot of road rage. To put the metaphor another way, courtesy of a Muslim friend: there are many roads to God, yet each of us thinks ours is the most direct. All our journeys to the same destination by a variety of paths are shared journeys anyway.

The people who have shared their stories here are not necessarily heroes or role models; that would be too easy. There was nothing otherworldly about these folks; they needed to sleep every night, eat every day, pay bills, and do laundry. In addition, some of the details in some of the stories may be a little hard to hear. People do bad things, dumb things, make serious mistakes. That's precisely why forgiveness is so radical, so liberating. Divine reconciliation would mean less if it embraced only the moderately flawed and left out the unsavory people most in need of saving. The biblical story of the prodigal son beautifully makes this point: when the older brother complains to his father that he ought to be praised, unlike his erring sibling, since he never caused his father grief, the father replies, "'Son, you are always with me, and all that is mine is yours. But we had to celebrate and rejoice, because this brother of yours was dead and has come to life; he was lost and has been found'" (Luke 15:31–32). The father's spiritual wisdom is timeless: it is always just and good to rejoice in transformation.

In choosing people who were willing to talk about their transformations, I also chose people who could "let their lives speak." Quakers—my religion—like to use this phrase to emphasize that we find God in experience, not in the sky. Their lives—many do service or otherwise find ways to share their message, one reason they agreed to talk to me, a stranger—were testimony and proof. Life deeds speak eloquently and louder than words, which can come too easy and make faith seem superficial. I considered what they *did* in addition to listening to what they *said*. Faith is supposed to make hard lives easier, but faith itself is not easy.

Listening requires a degree of faith in the speaker. To me it was natural to listen; some of the people I listened to were amazed that I would bother. To tell someone's story is to walk with them and bear witness. Like Mary Magdalene encountering the risen Jesus, a witness provides evidence that substantiates faith, the hope in things unseen.

Faith can be strengthened by skepticism, however. So I also questioned. To give context, corroboration, and other viewpoints, I also spoke to friends, colleagues, relations of the people I met—others who could bear witness as well as vouch for the credibility of, at times, incredible things. Because some of the histories I heard included others whose consent I would have needed in order to show connections, certain specifics that might provide explanation had to be omitted.

Sometimes, my questions were turned aside. It is not always pleasant to re-tell the past in searing detail. I trusted that the messages I heard were deepest and truest when freely given. I preferred cultivating trust to forcing answers.

Some argue that faith is a gamble. I could be wrong, but I think otherwise. This book is an album of snapshots at one brief point in complicated lives that have already rounded some strange bends. Skeptics would ask if jailhouse or foxhole religion is authentic; cynics would doubt it. Sometimes we must wait and see, and no one can tell the future. Certainly, those who have battled demons might be tempted again and succumb. So might you or I stumble on life's surprising journey. But with each stumble comes the choice of getting up again—or staying down.

When faith is new, it can be fragile. But tender young faith may paradoxically have the deepest of roots. By way of analogy, in 1998, I visited Mount Saint Helens, the Washington State volcano that had exploded eighteen years earlier. I saw the transformation of the earth that had been devastated by lava and hot ash—and what a landscape and lesson that was. The concentrated energy of destruction long spent, the quiet energy of renewal was abundantly underfoot, as the biome reknit a new diversity, tested by fire, on the slopes of a radically transformed mountain. A secret presence sometimes, life may be at once tenacious and tentative.

As I learned from Mount Saint Helens, so I learned, again and again, from these stories of faith found. To be changed, we simply stop trying to stubbornly determine our own ego-defined way. When we lower our defensive barricades, we invariably get a glimpse of another way. Change is not a product of self-will—not at all. Rather, it is a product of unconditioned grace if we but fling wide the window to let it in, let it be light in the darkness, as the poets of the Bible knew. People who find what they are meant to do find it because they let themselves be directed. Their first lesson is often humility. Change sticks when it is a transformation of spirit annealed by experience. I see a pattern in these lives, a pattern of surrender to the divine Spirit that frees the individual spirit to grow.

Yet God is often a very subtle quality in experience; by faith and work we bolster our ability to detect the divine. Think of the mustard seed. Think of God as the secret presence working within, as Thomas Kelly adjures. Think of God as an unseen atom, then look for God's presence as we do for atoms: look for traces of passage. Look for the tracks left by God. The best way to see God is to follow the footsteps of those who would follow God, to catch God in the act, in the actions of others.

In this book, I stand at the intersection of my experience and that of others. Each of the lives I was privileged to witness changed my own life by adding to my experience, confirming or challenging it, taking me to new places literally and figuratively, showing very different choices and possibilities. I went inside other people's living rooms and offices, and they showed me around their homes and their experiences.

The sharing of stories is one way to build the bonds of relationship that make up real community, a holding of things in common. Sharing stories is a lot like breaking bread: both of these activities sustain those who share. Thus, besides telling other people's stories, I include my own.

At the outset of this project, my husband told me I could not know where this would lead; this became true, literally and figuratively. His words came back to me as I began piling up the frequent-flyer miles. Unintended, my physical journey became a spiritual journey. I started this journey by looking for "subjects"; at its end, I felt I had found new perspective. Listening to stories of other people's healing journeys wrote a new chapter in my own history book.

I grew up in a household rocked periodically with emotional upheavals. My father had five breakdowns over the course of more than thirty years of shared family life. The diagnoses varied, but the cause seemed clear and unchanging: traumatic experiences as a medic in World War II. I am my father's daughter. I have had four episodes of significant emotional impairment, the most serious of which saw me psychiatrically hospitalized for three months in 1980.

Twenty years later, my spiritual development has brought me to the point of seeing the past anew, of re-remembering in order to revise not events, but their meaning. I have begun to reinterpret what I formerly described as "nervous breakdowns" as "spiritual crises." I have read psychology, spirituality, and health writers who say that pain is one powerful way of demanding attention. Crises offer chances to grow. They are gifts I didn't know I had received, because they came well disguised.

I came to this book looking for people who have made successful transformations of their childhood legacies, their mistakes, or their unexpected, unwanted emotional burdens of trauma or loss. I had a product—a book—as the goal, but as the process of the journey and the writing began to unfold, it involved and changed me. Everybody I met along the way told me they had looked within and there found healing balm, divinely given. But in the process of living and learning, they learned that the "answer" was not at the end of the road. Rather, the "answer" was the trip itself, a search honestly and humbly undertaken.

To tell my own story, I have sent "postcards" from stops along this transformational road. This seemed like a natural medium for a traveler to use to convey the sights and sounds of the present. The postcards also weave in selected episodes from my past. Sometimes the connection to prior events was very logical. When I revisited cities where I had been earlier in my life, I revisited memories. In other instances I have tried to link my traveler's impressions to themes and events of my past. The postcards follow my life's chronology, selecting and reflecting on incidents beginning in childhood and continuing to the present.

Good Quaker that he is, Thomas Kelly observes that what we think is our own doing is actually only evidence of and testimony to the secret presence within. That indwelling presence sustains us and guides us. Like any good secret, it also surprises us. As we discover we are far more than we once thought in our abjectness, life becomes sweet and rich.

One of my favorite metaphors for the unique richness of the recycled life comes from Raymond Carver, himself a remarkably gifted recovering alcoholic who became one of the most influential short-story writers in recent times. With his gift for saying things quickly and memorably, he also wrote some economical and exquisite poetry. One of his poems serves up the metaphor of something rich and simple—just like icing

on the cake, a New Orleans lagniappe, or gravy on mashed
potatoes at life's banquet, to which we are graciously invited.

## Gravy

No other word will do. For that's what it was. Gravy.
Gravy, these past ten years.
Alive, sober, working, loving and
being loved by a good woman. Eleven years
ago he was told he had six months to live
at the rate he was going. And he was going
nowhere but down. So he changed his ways
somehow. He quit drinking! And the rest?
After that it was all gravy, every minute
of it, up to and including when he was told about,
well,
some things that were breaking down and
building up inside his head. "Don't weep for me,"
he said to his friends. "I'm a lucky man.
I've had ten years longer than I or anyone
expected. Pure Gravy. And don't forget it."

# PART I

# *Reversal*

# Anthony Hollins

*Grace moving*

> *No weapon that is fashioned against you*
> *shall prosper . . .*
> —Isaiah 54:17

Anthony Hollins's legs are the tools of his art.

His legs have been shaped into powerful muscles: long, taut thigh muscles, bulging, rounded calf muscles, articulated beneath smooth skin. Even at rest, those legs seem poised to move. More than flesh, blood, muscle, and bone, his legs are as much an artist's instrument as a writer's pen, a painter's brush.

Anthony can lift a leg skyward, point toe toward heaven, both legs forming a single, 180-degree line. His shaven head is part of the signature that is his body. He is flesh, animated by spirit, muscle, brain—all moving together to music.

In his art, he stretches the human form effortlessly into graceful new possibilities. In his life, Anthony is also exploring new possibilities.

The thirty-five-year-old Chicagoan is a dancer and chore-ographer, founder of church and community dance groups for youth in the Chicago area, and active in his church, Trinity United Church of Christ on Chicago's South Side. He is also engaged in work he didn't expect but has come to accept, like some unsought but ultimately divine anointing.

Anthony is waging a campaign for AIDS awareness in the African American church and community. "I didn't imagine I'd live my life as a poster child for AIDS," he says. But life regularly foils expectations, and Anthony yielded to a new sense of calling. "I said, 'Lord, you use me any way you want to.'"

On March 7, 1999, a World AIDS Day of Prayer, the Lord's agenda for Anthony included Holy Angels Church. Located in a middle-class, historic African American neighborhood known as Bronzeville, the church is shoehorned in on a residential street on Chicago's near Southeast Side. Inside, the walls bear divine street art, murals with scenes from the life of Jesus of the People. The look of the place—bold colors, folk-art-style iconography—yokes cultural and biblical sensibilities. This is a place where the gospel of the Lord must make street sense—be a true social gospel—if it is to make any sense at all, if it is to have any relevance to ordinary, everyday life lived on Chicago's streets.

From the pulpit, in booming tones, Rev. John Calicott, church pastor, grabs the congregation's attention for today's topic: AIDS among African Americans. The statistics are grim: as is the case with so many other American physical and social ills, African Americans are now experiencing a disproportionate share of new HIV infections and AIDS cases. Changing the face of AIDS from white and homosexual to black and heterosexual, African Americans now constitute the majority of new cases of the disease.

"It appears that in the African American community we wish to pretend this is not a reality," intones Calicott, underlining the verbs with his voice as if to shake his hearers out of denial. "The next big wave," the preacher goes on to warn, "will be teenagers who think they have been safe."

*Us?* Teenagers, sitting in pews and choir area, rustle and straighten to attention as youthful Anthony strides into the sanctuary to offer his testimony. His dark, double-breasted suit elegantly drapes his long, lean body.

Although not a preacher with a deep, resonant voice, Anthony gives a riveting message. His topic is AIDS and Jesus and healing the spirit. Jesus is at the center of Anthony's language; Jesus is at the center of Anthony's conversion. Anthony's Jesus reaches out to heal the sick, just as he did long ago. "There's power in that name," says Anthony. "That name has changed me on the inside."

Anthony outlines his life story for his listeners, relating the classic tale of a boy who grew up knowing he was "different": he was gay. As children will, his peers mocked his difference, burning on him the label "faggot," like a cruel brand. Beginning at age fifteen, he found dance to be a source of comfort and expression.

Anthony used other ways, too, to meet his needs, ways he calls—without detailing them—"addictive behaviors." Still, however, he didn't get the love and closeness he was looking for.

Instead, he got AIDS.

Shortly after he was diagnosed in 1996, Anthony grew ill, thin, and desperate; he wanted to die. Into that void rushed something old from childhood, something that had not abandoned him—although he had abandoned it—something sustaining, a place of refuge, a name to call on, to call out loud.

"The word of God sticks like glue," Anthony says. "I began to call that name: Jesus." And Jesus met the reprobate on the road and held out a hand in forgiveness.

That touch brought healing.

"Once I said, 'I have the AIDS virus,' I began to experience healing," Anthony says, continuing slowly with a statement that is especially difficult for him to make. "I thank God I have AIDS, because I am no longer the whore I was. God wants to forgive us, today."

Anthony then asks the congregation: "If God forgave you, why can't you forgive someone else?"

Forgiveness is balm for the pain of past mistakes. For Anthony, "Jesus saves" is more than a figure of speech: Jesus is an eternal lifeline, grabbed, tightly held. More, Jesus is also a brother, someone who can be approached with humility and familiarity. When Jesus is called, he will answer. Like a mantra, the name of Jesus can be called again and again, summoning power to get out of bed in the morning, to raise one's voice in praise.

This is no silent church. The congregation claps as the organ burbles tunes and the choir makes loud and joyful noise. Anthony's testimony is punctuated by amens and yes-Lords, signs the congregation makes of affirmation, of unity with their brother. When Anthony is finished, a few people leave their seats to embrace the prodigal son, to welcome him back to the safe arms of the Lord, as the gospel song holds. For as long as an embrace, Anthony has the warm acceptance his lonely boy self was looking for.

"Holy Angels praised God today," Calicott tells the congregation. "This is not just about AIDS."

In July 1999, Anthony is getting a big sendoff before he relocates to Atlanta, Georgia, where his mother and dad live and where he hopes new grass will offer peaceful green pastures. Inside Mr. G's Supper Club on Chicago's South Side, more than a hundred supporters are gathered to fete the dancer, thank him, pray for him, and enjoy a bountiful meal. A buffet table is groaning under steaming pans of chicken, ribs, potatoes, pasta, and bowls of salads, and pans of cakes. In the club, the lights cozily dimmed, the clink of glasses and silverware is percussion in a steady symphony of conversation, exclamations, and laughter. Gathered as if family, Anthony's fans and friends applaud a program that mixes effusive praise and expressive dance.

Six overall-clad boys stride to the center of the room, their movements combining the athletic energy of break dancing with the traditional grace of ballet steps, set to the music of "Hold On." They are one of five youthful troupes performing to honor their choreographer and teacher. After each company performs, they swarm to hug Anthony, who looks thin in a gauzy white shirt, but has his dancer's feet in a pair of shiny red shoes. Then, with a group of fifteen men, some of them relatively untutored, Anthony jumps in to lead his dancers in a signature piece, to follow the music of "No Weapon," to spread his dance message.

"He is our brother, he is our role model," says television news broadcaster Deloris MeBain, there to share with the crowd a videotape of Anthony's life story that is scheduled to air on Chicago television in the fall.

"Anthony, we let you go, but you are always with us," says Rose Jennings, a representative from the Youth Services Department in the far west exurban city of Aurora, where Anthony has mentored and choreographed the Aurora Youth Dance Company.

Amber Sanders has close-cropped hair and the limbs of a classical nymph, solid, coiled with potential energy. She tells the group how seven years dancing with Anthony's New Life Performance Company has transformed her, taken her to Atlanta, Philadelphia, and "just about every church in Chicago" for dance ministry. A student at Barat College, Amber will major in and pursue her career in dance. The talent is from

God; the discipline something Anthony helped her to develop. Doors to other worlds of experience are standing open for her.

"It's amazing," this young woman marvels, "how you realize just how much you touch people."

Atlanta doesn't work out as Anthony had hoped, so by early 2000, he is back in Chicago, looking for a job and trying to stay healthy and make ends meet.

Living with God's mystery means living with ambiguity and frustration. Living with the AIDS virus means living with physical and spiritual vulnerability. The calendar can be a long string of down days, down weeks. AIDS is just one more problem added to the list of daily problems of washing the dishes and getting food on the table.

Anthony has a hard time finding a job. Everyone is happy to have his services, hear his powerful story, be inspired by his gravity-defying motion, feel good for free. But paying him? *Well, we'll check the budget. We'll give you a call back.* So it goes through half a dozen job interviews with AIDS service groups, all of which turn him down: *No thanks.*

This gets frustrating, and Anthony's voice reflects his impatience. Being in service to God is clear—but what God wants done is not. If it's your will, Lord, then what is your will? A little light on this question, and how do I get that light bill paid, by the way?

Anthony may be faithful but, like Job, he is tried. He experiences depression. There is a sense sometimes, as he puts it: "Is there hope left and if so what the hell is it?" The answer to the question is the difference between staying in bed and getting up. As a volunteer living with AIDS, Anthony knows a lot of people with terminal illnesses. But he tries to stay focused on living with AIDS, on living. "We don't want to be stuck living in death" is how he puts it.

It's tough to keep giving and giving and giving hope and inspiration and not getting anything back, especially when there's the light bill to pay. How Anthony pays those bills is never completely clear, although he has many friends and relatives. By summer, though, he has a job with the Chicago Park District.

Anthony's creative energy keeps him going to dance engagements. He and photographer Donnell Collins are also collaborating on a photo project that could be an exhibit or a book or both: "The Faces of AIDS" will show the men, the women, the young, the old, the straight, the gay. The photos are portraits of people living with AIDS, gay and straight couples, a son and his parents. They are people who have let down their guards, who have permitted the camera a look inside, who have said, *Come in to my house. I may not live next door but I am your neighbor, even if you aren't aware of me. Even if, as Peter did Jesus, you deny me. Even if you marginalize me. Even if you hate me, I am your neighbor.*

In keeping with his mission to raise awareness, Anthony's intention is to focus on AIDS in the black community. "Jesus went to visit the sick," says Anthony. "Churches are still in denial about the reality of AIDS—and we call ourselves Christian."

Anthony is also writing meditations on God's will and the demon of depression. The journal is a space for self-talk, for self-listening, for trying to hear that still small voice whispering the reason to get up in the morning and face another day. Much will be given, but it may well not be what you ask for. It will be the gift of AIDS, not the gift of fame or fortune. It will be the prism of mortality, which focuses exclusively on what is most important.

Anthony gets grace from God. He gets—and gives—care at the CORE Center, a freestanding, one-stop clinic for the treatment of infectious diseases on Chicago's near West Side. The CORE Center is part of the "Hospital City" complex of teaching and public-health facilities that sprawl just west of the city's downtown, in an area that is home to Cook County Hospital, a quintessential public urban health-care institution that even looks the part: grey, massive, and aging.

The CORE Center opened in 1998, the first of its kind to bring together what's needed to treat and prevent HIV/AIDS and other communicable diseases that spread too readily through medically and economically disadvantaged urban communities. The center provides outpatient treatment and services, and houses research and education programs. Inpatients go right next door when necessary—to the county hospital.

"When I go visit people on the AIDS ward, they're so hopeless," Anthony says. "But there's hope in friends, in relationships. You can see possibilities that are unimaginable."

In addition to getting care at the CORE Center, Anthony volunteers there several times a week. "Whatever you give to the universe is exactly what you get back," he says. "You have to be able to give hope to get hope back."

Anthony works under Volunteer Services Director Phyllis L. Rodgers. "The role that Anthony and other volunteers play is to be there in time of need," says Phyllis, who has worked for Cook County health facilities since 1991, when the public mostly saw AIDS victims as white, male, and gay. A lot of CORE patients are African-American, female, heterosexual, and mothers of young children. Rodgers was the first African-American hired to do AIDS case management.

Phyllis has the energy of indignation and determination but is not unstoppable. She apologizes; this is a day for her to be tired and sad, she says. Goes with the territory. "It's only by faith that I'm here," she says. "Everything that I do is by faith. I don't know anything else." She then adds, "Grace and mercy shall follow you through."

Phyllis has come to see and know that which she couldn't have imagined in her previous career as an investment banker at one of Chicago's larger banks. "I was a clone," she says with a laugh. "One day we came to work and we all had the same things on." She fled the corporate world, but kept the skills she honed.

"I was in rehearsal for this," she says. Her little office is no bank boardroom with cherry wainscoting and leather chairs that roll easily on thick carpet. Rather, the CORE Center has given her a functional closet of a room crammed with reams and stacks of papers and boxes, a cluttered desk, walls and shelves papered with flyers, calendar, posters—not many chairs or elbowroom for visitors. On the computer is a decorative screen saver: a ballerina. The girl can dance.

"Some people take the diagnosis [as] 'this is the end,'" Phyllis notes. "Others say this is the best thing that ever happened to them. The diagnosis for some people becomes a new beginning."

♻

Each time I see Anthony over the course of two years, I scan his face anxiously. Saying to someone with AIDS, "How are you?" is to ask a loaded question. Each time I see him, he appears thinner; there are more hollows and shadows appearing in his body. I see fluctuating energy levels, but some power still stokes his furnace, gets him out of bed in the morning.

The same power gets him out of the hospital. Late in the summer of 2000, a year after his warm sendoff to Atlanta, Anthony is hospitalized for six days, diagnosed with a stomach ulcer aggravated by stress. Getting sick can be hell for someone with AIDS: How sick will you get this time? How will health-care personnel respond to someone with AIDS? Social prejudice can be gauged through the degree of reluctance to touch.

Certainly, facing a bill for $1,600 in medications in the wake of his hospitalization is stressful for Anthony. "I might as well die," he says with grim humor to a friend to whom he is reciting some of the details of his latest hospitalization and the price of living with AIDS. Fortunately, someone in Anthony's network comes through with appropriate medication that costs only $695 a bottle. Stress! $695 a bottle!

Anthony is more settled in his South Side home since he returned from Atlanta earlier this year. His living room is white and glass: overstuffed white sofa, white carpet, white blinds filtering daylight, glass-topped tables that hold photo collections. His home, in fact, is a veritable photo gallery. Framed photos are massed on every table surface and decorate a room divider: friends, family, lots of smiling kids, Anthony's many dancers. Two stuffed bears, one a Winnie the Pooh—a favorite of Anthony's—guard one cluster of photos. Two pair of Anthony's shoes sit neatly near the stairs.

Dance is the other motif in his house. Prints, paintings, and pictures of dancers are hung everywhere. He is also fond of candles; lit in his cool white living room on an overcast Sunday afternoon, they cast rich pools of light on his smooth dark skin, on the meticulously clean-shaven dome that is his head.

The candles also provide light for photos. Although Anthony is not feeling terribly well and has only been home one day from the hospital, he has the energy to do another shoot in the photo project with his collaborator, photographer

Donnell Collins. Anthony recruits the subjects, all of whom are African Americans living with AIDS, and "choreographs" the shoot, suggesting poses for the subjects. Collins fires off frame after frame, prowling around the subjects, seeking new angles and possibilities.

John is one of the "new faces of AIDS." Anthony was impressed when he heard John's testimony—the latter's revelation that he lives with the AIDS virus—in a room full of African American men at a church. "To stand in front of a bunch of black men and say 'I have this' is not easy," Anthony insists. That is one reason Anthony is determined to do his work of making AIDS in the African American community more visible, less deniable, more a matter of caring for "my brother."

The photo shoot with John is in Jackie Robinson Park, a Chicago Park District neighborhood park with a gem of a baseball field and stands, near Anthony's South Side home. John is a tall, solid man, somewhere in his thirties, with beautifully sculpted limbs and a serious expression on his face. It takes a little jiving from Anthony to get John to break into a grin.

John sits, relaxed, arm stretched out on the back of the bench in the covered wooden grandstand, letting Anthony direct various poses. He looks dead-on into the camera, unsmiling—the camera probing beneath his surface and the five-o'clock summer sun backlighting him. John's clothes are neatly pressed, his new athletic shoes unsullied by dirt or wear.

For a second photo, Anthony has scouted out another location. It has a bridge, per a request from photographer Collins, who wants to use a bridge in a visual motif. The wooden footbridge is one of the distinctive features of the Osaka Japanese Garden, located behind the Museum of Science and Industry in Jackson Park.

The gardens, surrounded by a fence, contain sculptured trees, small Japanese-style shady wooden enclosures for sitting, and a pond, traversed by the wooden arched bridge. The pond is urban-beautiful, filled with the green pads of water lilies—and a protruding green neck of a beer bottle.

Doubling his presence, the pond reflects Anthony's figure, as the day drips with Chicago summer humidity. As he carefully blots the glistening dots of sweat that appear on his shaved head, Anthony assumes pose after pose, one leg soaring skyward, the other anchored on the ground, forming nearly a 180-degree straight line of leg. This is candid Anthony, in his element, his art. He is a performer, not a talker. What he has to say, he says with his body.

Anthony didn't tell friends at his church that he was hospitalized. They would have come to visit, he explains, "and I did not want people to see me in that condition."

Anthony is careful, even reticent, about what he shows and shares of himself and to whom. For example, he won't share explicit information about his past; he won't share certain details about how he used to live, saying he prefers to focus on other things. "I used to be the same person that I am," he says, "but I had to grow into it." He refuses to play hero; he is simply a man blessed with creativity and given a great burden, hoping to touch a few lives.

News about someone living with AIDS has only a slim possibility of being surprising. After all, it is a disease with a known outcome, although time and quality of life are key variables that people with the illness try to maximize.

Anthony succeeds in surprising me. He's choreographing yet another Martin Luther King Day celebration in my hometown of Aurora, Illinois, the event at which we originally met.

That's become routine. It's his love that is fresh and new—and his soul's partner is a woman.

This new development adds another twist to his human story, taking it in yet another direction that astonishes him. He understands this new love in his life as a revelation that occurred after he stopped seeing his God as a God with limits. "I struggled for many years with the issue of sexuality, never could even hear that I was going to meet my soul's connection, let alone that it would be a woman." But she is—and she is a singer. He hopes to make beautiful music with her.

"Our test evolves into our testimony," Anthony says in that phrase-turning way of his.

As for myself, I need to call a halt to information gathering; book and life meet and part company arbitrarily.

"My story continues," Anthony says.

# Max Bonnin
## *Walking the good earth*

*He makes me lie down in green pastures;*
*he leads me beside still waters;*
*   he restores my soul.*

—Psalm 23:2–3

It's so dark on Church Road in rural northwest Mississippi that I miss my turn for Bonne Terre, an upscale country inn built by Max and June Bonnin. The sign is lit, but it's small. Max, whom I am meeting, says that if people want to find him, they will—and if they don't, they won't. Bonne Terre's one hundred acres are secluded but accessible, only twenty minutes from the rest of the busy world via Memphis International Airport.

I drive a winding entry road onto the grounds, and the first thing I see is a chapel. This country inn has a chapel, an unusual amenity. A light bathes the building so that I can see its simple outline, stark against surrounding dark.

The place is clearly inhabited—lights and a row of parked cars give silent testimony—but outside, in the dark and cold December air, all is still. Then, apparition-like, something approaches. It's only knee-level, though, turning out to be a golden retriever, snuffling around me with mildness and curiosity. I take it as a welcome and exchange a greeting with this well-mannered dog. (The next day I am formally introduced to Kailee, one of three resident dogs—the others are Bailey, another retriever, and Chelsea, a cocker spaniel.)

Gravel crunching under my feet, my breath visible in the night air, I see enough of generously proportioned white buildings and acres of shining dark (that is probably a lake) to be as curious as a character in an enchanted tale. I go inside the main house, where a key to my room—the Heather Room—is courteously waiting in an envelope with my name on it. A decorated Christmas tree adds a cheery touch. It feels more like coming to visit relatives than checking in for overnight lodging. I'm looking forward to meeting the master of this Southern manor.

Escorted to my room, I wonder if I have ascended an oak stairway to heaven. Certainly it is a haven from the hum of all things ordinary. The door—a little sign on it says "Heather," distinguishing it from the adjoining "Periwinkle" and "Rose" rooms, which are painted their namesake colors—is open, and welcoming light beckons me inside. I almost gasp at the size and sight of a huge, barge-like queen-size bed that turns out to have a featherbed lurking beneath its thick floral spread, lace-trimmed sheets, and pile of pillows. Potted plants offer living hospitality, French doors offer access to a porch, a fireplace painlessly turns on with a switch, a Jacuzzi in the bathroom promises relaxation, and two thick, white terry bathrobes embroidered with "Bonne Terre" hang from a hook on the bathroom door. Also hanging in a frame on the peach-colored wall of the Heather Room is the story of Bonne Terre (French for "good earth"), the dream of Max and June Bonnin.

Max met June in 1989 in Memphis and proposed to her two days after they met. Blue-eyed, curly-haired Max was a successful executive in health-care sales for big companies; he traveled the West Coast and had homes in several different cities. Blue-eyed, blonde June was a successful businesswoman in commercial leasing; she traveled the East Coast. They married in Paris in 1989, and their blond, blue-eyed daughter, Ashley, was born in 1990. Max and June were fixing to live comfortably ever after.

Five years later, however, the happiness express ground to a stop. In 1994, June was diagnosed with lymphoma. She was given six months to live.

"I had always been able to figure out anything," says Max, reflecting on his response to June's health crisis. "When all of a sudden your spouse is given six months to live, you can't figure that out." A new and wholly different way was needed.

The treatment June opted for was holistic. She eschewed chemotherapy and radiation and, instead, made a lifestyle change, altering her diet and her whole way of being. She and Max prayed and turned the situation, and their lives, over to God. "I think a lot of people find the Lord as a result of a trying time," Max says.

Part of Max and June's lifestyle change included realizing their shared dream: building and operating a country inn, a dream they had drawn from their separate but mutual experiences of staying at inns and bed-and-breakfasts while traveling on business. From a strictly business point of view, it was a little bit visionary, but Max and June were business people who now had a vision. You get an idea, then you come up with ways to implement it. Max describes their plan in the straightforward way that probably helped convince local banks to lend them lots of money to finance the purchase and construction of the inn in a one-hundred-acre cow pasture.

"The banks were surprised when we went in for the money," he recalls. Had they ever owned a hotel? Nope, the

Bonnins told the bankers. Ever operated a restaurant? No again.

"June and I—we just never were afraid of following our hearts," Max continues. "If I say I'm going to do something, I'll do it." Good credit histories, he adds, were also helpful in obtaining the financing they needed.

And so the dream came true: Bonne Terre Country Inn and Café, which June designed, opened on Labor Day 1996. The restaurant quickly earned praise from the *Memphis Commercial Appeal*, the local paper, and *Memphis* magazine. Bonne Terre was featured in 1998 in *Southern Living*, the regional magazine of all things fine and Southern. Wines on the inn's list top out at $600 for a 1995 Chateau Mouton Rothschild, and dinner possibilities may include grilled spice-rubbed quail, lemon and ginger-crusted salmon with wasabi aioli, and rack of Australian lamb.

The inn has fifteen rooms, all of which enjoy a view of one of two five-acre lakes. Rimmed by mature trees now wearing the rusted-out foliage of very late autumn, the lakes have fountains illuminated at night, adding one of many continental European accents of ambience. Max and June had lived in Europe, though June had Southern roots.

The exterior face of the buildings is white wood, columned Greek revival, very Southern-country-home to my Northern eye. Trellised walkways covered with gnarly vines—the seasonal skeletons of climbing roses and wisteria—connect the buildings. Flowers are still blooming in this middle-South location in early December. Bright multicolored pansies, harlequin-like, are tolerating the nippy weather. The rosebushes succumbed to frost only two weeks earlier; some yellow roses linger on a tall bush, the flowers beautifully shaped but discolored, freeze-dried versions of their in-season beauty.

Wearing a fleece-lined jacket over his dark denim shirt, Max tells me that I've just missed the roses. We're sipping late morning coffee in the bright, windowed, oak-floored, stone-and-brick-walled café. He's already been on the go since 6:30 this morning, having taken Ashley to school and worked out, two of the activities that start his day. Max is proud of how the property has turned out and continues to unfold; he's also bird-dogging a lot of details that add up to making things right. He carries with him a portfolio filled with papers and a planner.

As we talk, Max keeps apologizing and excusing himself to attend to business. There are problems with windows ordered for a three-hundred-seat reception and special events hall—to be named Ashley Hall, after the youngest Bonnin—and the bricklayers are ready and waiting; the restaurant is open seven days a week; the inn has a conference center; Bonne Terre has been the site for 150 marriages; December is the season for enticing couples for a deluxe New Year's celebration. If it isn't one thing, it's another.

"My days fly by, my weeks fly by," Max says.

Bonne Terre came from a dream, and is meant to nurture dreaming. But Max and June's shared dream came to an end on March 15, 1999. June, whose cancer was in remission, was a passenger aboard Amtrak's storied City of New Orleans liner when it collided outside Bourbonnais, Illinois, with a trailer-truck laden with more than thirty-five tons of steel. When fourteen-car train met steel-burdened truck at almost eighty miles per hour at a crossing where, according to testimony, warning lights and bells were activated, June was in the sleeper near the front of the train. Her daughter, Ashley, was with her, as well as her eleven-year-old granddaughter, Jessica Tickle Whitaker, and two friends, Rainey Lipscomb, ten, and Lacey

Lipscomb, eight, sisters and neighbors of the Bonnin family. The girls had been having a pajama party. The neighboring families—close friends—were returning from a spring-break trip to Chicago, where the girls had delighted in a visit to the American Girl doll store.

The collision sent a second engine into the sleeper car, slicing the car, spilling diesel fuel, and igniting fires that burned the wreckage. Ashley was found outside the sleeping car by Amtrak chef Mark George; part of her right leg had to be amputated. The other three girls died with June; they were among eleven passengers killed in one of the worst accidents in Amtrak's history. The magnitude of the crash assured immediate national headlines, and the controversy over the role played by the driver of the truck continued for months, leaving unresolved questions about the traumatic event.

So the small chapel on the grounds at Bonne Terre—which had been in the plans for the complex all along—became a memorial chapel when it was dedicated on February 24, 2000. The chapel is small, spare, and always open, scaled for individual contemplation rather than collective worship. Inside, vertical cypress beams direct the eye upward, and a cross blends into the wall's wooden face. On another wall at the front of the chapel is a large painting in blue hues showing the figure of Jesus in the clouds with three children and a woman. On one side of Jesus are June Bonnin and her granddaughter, Jessica; on the other are Rainey and Lacey Lipscomb.

Max leaves the chapel unlocked; he also lets local churches use it for various functions. A big prayer service has taken place the evening before my arrival, and two college students, Jesse and Melissa, return to the chapel while I am there. Jesse is praying for a miracle for his uncle, who has cancer. Melissa offers prayers of thanksgiving; God has helped her heal, she believes, from a serious auto accident.

"God is getting ready to do something awesome," says Jesse, his Mississippi accent emphasizing *awesome*. I look at the picture of June and I open the Bible in the pew to read about Job and his suffering.

"Around God is awesome majesty" (Job 37:22). God is always awesome, but Job and others come to know that God is hard to explain, impossible to predict, and never on schedule.

People have vastly different ways of talking about God, to God. Jesse tells me the prayer meeting was exciting because people were speaking in tongues, one of the gifts of the Spirit, spoken about by the apostle Paul. A stained-glass window in the chapel features the Holy Spirit in the center, encircled by eight tongues of fire.

Max says he's had three or four crystal-clear examples of being spoken to directly by the Holy Spirit. Two of them occurred the night of the train wreck. Having been notified of the accident, Max raced into the night to southern Illinois in a caravan with his neighbor Mat Lipscomb (Rainey and Lacey's dad) and Kelley Whitaker (June's daughter from a previous marriage and also Jessica's mother). Torn between dread and hope, the anxious party received calls from the crash scene as information emerged from the chaos of the wreck hundreds of miles away. Ashley had been located; June had not.

Then Max heard this, not on the phone: "Max, June's with me now. She's not here." And in this direct and mysterious way, Max already knew his wife's fate when, after an eight-hour drive, he arrived at the hospital in Bourbonnais where Ashley had been taken. The hospital was thronged with medical personnel and families of train passengers; 116 people had been injured in the crash and needed care.

As Max made his way through the crowd of all those abruptly linked by common catastrophe, he heard a voice again: "Max, this is me. This is love. These are my children." And

God's children—medical personnel, neighbors, people he met in the long days that followed—helped Max care for his child as she recovered from surgery and her injuries.

Almost two years later, Max says he's serene most of the time. Between raising his daughter and taking care of business, he makes sure to stay busy—pointing out that he lost a business partner as well as his wife.

For business, social, and spiritual reasons, Max spends a lot of time talking with those who stay at his and June's country inn. Guests arrive from all over—fifteen percent of the clients come from overseas—and they learn the history of Bonne Terre from the story that is posted in every room. In doing so, they come to understand the agony beneath the tranquility.

"They read the story, they walk the grounds here," says Max. "When they leave, it's like I've known them forever."

Max makes friends; Max relies on friends. One friend, Jerry Gooch, a cardiovascular surgeon, has watched the changes in Max, the changes in Max's life. Max calls on his friend for support. "All we can do is be there and answer the page," Gooch says. "We can't replace the things that are gone."

Gooch first met Max and June when June was referred to him for a complication of her lymphoma. "I remember talking with her and Max in the treatment room, and we spoke of the opportunity to express the faith we had and how God could intervene in situations," Gooch recalls. "We had a strong belief that God could change things."

Max is still driven by the same ambition that made him a successful businessman, but it's different now, Gooch says of his friend. "The lifestyle he walks now is so totally counter to what he did for so many years in the business world."

A little detail testifies to just how different. Max, for so many years a performer in the high-power corporate arena before he and June made their lifestyle change and came to

Memphis, had to buy a suit for his wife's funeral. He no longer owned one.

"He didn't dress up anymore," says Gooch. "He got rid of everything."

Max has more business plans. While Bonne Terre is a big, bustling enterprize for one man to oversee, Max hopes to extend his operations. A construction road east of Bonne Terre is the current entrance to what will eventually be a gated community of forty homes surrounding Bonne Terre. Max says the homes, which will have access to the grounds of Bonne Terre as well as its restaurant, are intended to sell in the $400,000 to $500,000 range. Northern Mississippi outside Memphis is growing, he observes.

But Max is not the same businessman he was ten years ago, before June was diagnosed with cancer and the couple began a spiritual journey that Max continues. "I was driven by money," says the former sales executive, "and I was miserable."

Now, years of love and loss later, the experts he consults on important business decisions include the Lord. "I pray about things before I do them," he says. "Boy, that works well. God expects you to be focused, but to keep him in mind for direction."

♻

The Lipscomb family met the Bonnin family when both were building in the same area in DeSoto County, in the tip-top corner of northwest Mississippi where a small-town lawyer named John Grisham once practiced. The families' friendship developed naturally, since they had so much in common: age, business backgrounds, and girls close in age. And like Max and June, Cindy Lipscomb had given up a high-power, high-paying job—hers was in retail management. The work she opted for was mothering and, like June, she was an older mom. She'd had her girls, Rainey, Lacey, and Jesse Anne, in her thirties, having married Mat Lipscomb when she was thirty-two.

When June wasn't feeling well—for a while she battled a brain tumor—Cindy would just add Ashley to her team of daughters, taking her to whatever lesson or appointment was scheduled. The girls attended the same school and went to camp together. "Lots of times you'd see me with four girls," says Cindy. Cindy could even pitch in at Bonne Terre; her retail background came in handy with product selection for the gift shop.

So it was natural for all of them to go on spring-break vacation together in 1999. They had done it the year before, visiting Florida together. With their families mingled so, their fates mingled, too.

Cindy didn't realize what had taken place when the wreck occurred the night of March 15, 1999. She and her youngest daughter, Jesse Anne, then five, were in a sleeper at the other end of the train, with Cindy's mother, Sudie Davis. "Where we were, we shook and shook," she recalls. "We thought we had derailed. We never heard the explosion." All three of them were uninjured.

Faith got Cindy through the funeral of two of her young daughters; faith gets her out of bed. She is convinced that Rainey and Lacey are in heaven, a place so wonderful that it's beyond conceiving—"What no eye has seen, nor ear heard, nor the human heart conceived, what God has prepared for those who love him" (1 Corinthians 2:9)—and equally convinced that the family members will be together again after death. "If we did not know beyond a shadow of a doubt that we would be reunited, I just don't know how I would live otherwise," she says. Having Jesse Anne to care for has become a heightened blessing.

"I would be in so much of a bigger hurry if they were all three up there," says Cindy.

Cindy and June had already shared their faith walk through June's illness. "She was battling her cancer and we prayed about her brain tumor," Cindy says. "When we saw God stop that in its tracks . . . she was definitely one who would build your faith."

Even before she lost her two daughters, Cindy worked at nurturing her prayer life, trying to weave it more seamlessly into her days, trying to "pray without ceasing" (1 Thessalonians 5:17). She and Jesse Anne sometimes pray together, for example, before one of Jesse Anne's stage performances. (At seven, Jesse Anne is becoming a stage trouper, following her big sisters' footsteps.)

Cindy has also found a voice to speak to people. Much to her amazement, she finds herself spending time as a public speaker, sharing the story of her experience with other groups. She has lost both fear and dislike of speaking in public; rather, when she speaks, she experiences "God's peace." She remembers a time not too long before the accident when she and June were together and June was preparing to speak to a group about her experience of illness and healing. That memory made Cindy realize that she, too, had a story to share; it would be about raising children.

"This is not the story I wanted," Cindy says—but it is one that puts her in mind of Romans 8:28: "We know that all things work together for good for those who love God." And she tells Jesse Anne, who has at times wished to join her big sisters in heaven, "Maybe there are some people that God wants us to tell about Jesus before we go. Maybe there are some things we need to do before we go."

On Sundays, Mat, Cindy, and Jesse Anne worship with Max and Ashley at Christ United Methodist Church in Memphis and then attend Bible study. Afterward they go out for brunch. It's become a Sunday routine for the intertwined families.

Cindy observes that her neighbor has undergone great spiritual growth since the train wreck claimed his wife's life. "Max would probably admit to you that June was the spiritual head of the household [at first], but the accident caused him to move to a new level in his spiritual walk."

Max's friend Jerry Gooch agrees. "They were very much 'in the world,' and then they made this change to come back to Nesbit, Mississippi," the surgeon says of Max and June. "I think they could see God moving in their lives, [helping them] to feel like that's where they were supposed to be."

Besides having God "in his culture," as Max puts it, he is also close to his daughter. "Everybody loves Ashley," he says, paternal pride written large on his smiling face. As Max drives his daughter to school in nearby Olive Branch each morning, the child prays—and Max gets an idea of what's on her young mind. For a brief time after the accident, Ashley saw a counselor, but eventually persuaded her father that it was neither necessary nor helpful. "Dad," she complained, "all the counselor wants me to do is make collages and cry. Why not give me $150 [the counselor's fee] and I'll make collages at home?"

Like father, like daughter. "She wants to go into hotel and restaurant management," Max says of his fifth-grader. She doesn't like school, but she likes and plays volleyball, prosthesis notwithstanding. "She scored half the points in the championship game," her father assures me. Ashley and Max have baseball gloves for frequent games of catch. They took the gloves along on a Christmas trip to New York and father and daughter played catch in Central Park.

Ashley also likes animals; Max says the three dogs, ten cats, one lop-eared rabbit, and three horses constitute the Bonne Terre petting zoo. Ashley introduces me to Oreo; the rabbit lives in a little hutch outside the Bonne Gifts shop and is all black-and-white fur and floppy ears. Oreo submits to petting while she wriggles her mobile nose, eager to get back to the carrot chunk she is methodically whittling down.

The spirit of June is everywhere on the grounds, Max says. A picture of her and Max hangs by the entrance to the restaurant. Max is in black tie; June is a glowing picture of health, her blond head close to his. The photo was taken at a charity event five months before she died; it is the last picture of the two of them.

"The tranquility of Bonne Terre is the grace and gentle spirit June left there," reads a poem written by a friend in elegant calligraphy and hung on the wall of the main house at Bonne Terre. The halls of the main house are decked for the holidays. Also hung on the wall is a picture of June and a younger version of Ashley, another family photo that says "home" instead of "hotel."

I sit in the windowed end of the café, overlooking one of the lakes, and drink coffee and atmosphere. Birds are everywhere—sparrows, cardinals, a tufted titmouse—hip-hopping, hunting amid oak-leaf debris on the ground, availing themselves of the earth's hospitality to fuel themselves for winter. It looks as though some of them have taken up winter residence in the purple martin bird-apartment on the lakeshore. They are doing their job, playing their bit part as Bonne Terre wildlife, their part as the sparrows of the field.

I notice two hefty geese waddling along the shore of the lake; these guys are not birds of the field. Max says these gourmet geese ravaged his organic lettuce patch. He'll do it differently next growing season, inferring the lesson from experience.

Max has always been pretty decisive. "If I had my mind made up, there was no stopping me." His marriage proposal to June two days after they met is a case in point. "She said, 'What took you so long?'" he recounts with a laugh. "When it's right, it's right."

It may be right, but it isn't exactly what we want all of the time. June's illness taught the two of them that lesson. As it turned out, June overcame the illness that was expected to claim her and was given several more years, enough time to make the dream of Bonne Terre, precipitated by her cancer, come true. Yet, there was no holding onto that dream, no way of ensuring that best-laid plans and fond expectations will come to be.

No, Max says, he never thought about getting angry with God. "Gosh, no. This was all part of his plan."

The hard-won serenity of Bonne Terre is there for sharing. In fact, Max likes to promote it as a place for weddings and anniversaries, where couples and families can celebrate love—and can stay in love. Max and June's own abiding love is captured somehow in the very air of the place, reenacted somehow at the weddings that take place in the memorial chapel, a place of love and memory. Every leaf, every drop of water in the lakes, every brick of Bonne Terre, offers silent testimony to a larger love and peace enfolding those who live there, those who come there.

"The Holy Spirit made it clear that Bonne Terre is my mission here," Max continues. "I'll use the time and the peace within Bonne Terre as a centerpiece to witness for him."

I look through the nearby window. A scarlet cardinal lands on a tree branch, pauses a moment, and is off again, an arc of moving color in the drab of December. When it's right, it's right.

# Postcard

*Memphis*

Elvis Presley's Memphis is the name of a restaurant, but they might as well rename the whole city, it is so filled with memorials. Heartbreak Hotel is a convenient place to stay while paying homage at Graceland, the rock 'n' roll pioneer's homey li'l museum-estate. Elvis Presley Boulevard—street or avenue wouldn't do to honor the King—forms a major north-south thoroughfare here. Naturally, it goes past Graceland, which functions as a shrine for devotees who insist that Elvis isn't really dead.

I only get as close as the exit sign for Graceland, being too busy to stop and pay my pop-culture respects to the man who did so much to usher in the socially subversive triumvirate of sex, drugs, and rock 'n' roll. Not visiting Graceland in Memphis—the King's home away from home in the latter and fatter stages of his career—is a lot like not gambling while you're in Las Vegas. It's positively un-American; after the White House, Graceland is the most visited home in the country.

Memphis is also home to another cultural pioneer, Federal Express, a company that helped speed up our work lives, if not all the expectations we have about how quickly anything can happen. A quick fix used to suffice. Now it's gotta happen overnight—positively, absolutely.

By contrast, the speed of personal change, which I chronicle in this book, is almost glacial. A mistake can be made in the time it takes to pull a trigger, but it takes far more time, a lifetime's worth, to let go, to forgive, to practice living in a way that is neither destructive nor self-destructive. Elvis, for one, never figured it out.

# 1962

When I was a child, Elvis was a big star: young, but big. It was his late early period, when he made movie after movie. In 1962, around the time when Elvis' film *Follow That Dream* was popular, I was nine and scared. As children will, I was starting to ask big questions. I felt paralyzed by anxious fear for the state of my soul, gripped by a moral obsessive-compulsiveness that required laundering my soul as I might wash my hands. I was sure I was in sin all the time—and I could be calmed only by talking with a priest. Surely I would go straight to flaming and eternal perdition were I to die.

So I spent a lot of time walking back and forth, along three Chicago blocks, to the parish rectory, where priests lived their mysterious existence, basking in God's favor and magically dispensing it to the worthy. Outside the rectory, which wore a coat of bricks dark as a priest's garment, grew a redbud that donned beautiful purple blossoms in spring. I was taught that it was the Judas tree, the tree from which the treacherous apostle hanged himself in despair. Beauty and perfidy yoked: I tried to picture

Judas, who first betrayed God and then himself, out on a fatal tree limb. I missed the irony that the Judas tree was planted outside a rectory. Who was guilty?

Walking home from confession and pastoral conversation, I invariably felt lighter and purer. I would soothe myself by singing songs from the musical *West Side Story*, which energized me. I was back in the land of grace.

I spoke very little about my fears, although my mother knew that I was going through a difficult period. For many years afterward, I dismissed this as a small and embarrassing "holy-roller" interlude in my life. Later, when I began seeing a pattern in my life of periodic upheaval and distress, like the pattern that characterized my father's acute episodes, these times grew more significant and less odd and shameful.

I look back now and see fear overwhelming a sensitive child. I look back and see where some of my anger about organized religion started. I look back and see the God of my childhood, who was busy sternly saying, "Thou shalt not" and frightening children like some old neighborhood crank. I look back and see this mystery: Why do children suffer? Why are some molested, others beaten, others mentally tormented?

"We also boast in our sufferings, because we know that suffering produces endurance, and endurance produces character, and character produces hope, and hope does not disappoint us . . ." (Romans 5:3–5). Hope is a product of change, and it too proceeds slowly, growing from the ground of suffering, mysteriously carrying an antidote to suffering, in much the same way illness triggers the body to begin its own healing. Birth is pain, but it's the admission charge to life on the planet. We came crying hither. They sing the blues on Beale Street in Memphis. Elvis knew that, and his genius preserved the heart of longing and lamentation, even while liberating the energy within the music and transforming it.

I'm told that Memphis is especially pretty in the spring, when the dogwood blooms. The redbud—the Judas tree—blooms then, too. The whole city parties the first weekend of May, for a festival known as Memphis in May. But this is December, the trees are bare, and I'm flying by on an interstate highway, one of those American institutions that has helped homogenize the experience of different cities.

I have a habit of singing in the car, but I can't find a decent station on the rental-car radio. Dang! This town calls itself the birthplace of rock 'n' roll and the home of the blues.

Coming home became another story with a moral. I left my wallet in Atlanta, or it went missing there in the world's largest airport, as bottomless as the ocean for things lost or stolen. Unfortunately, I didn't discover that until airborne above Chicago, when I went to fish out my parking-lot ticket and realized that I was a victim of my own carelessness or someone else's dishonesty.

At 1:00 a.m., snow on the ground, I was cashless, driver's license-less, credit card-less, parking-lot ticket-less, and ready to sing the blues. My consumer, photo-ID'ed self was missing. I swore, I cried. Hope whispered in my ear: *Welcome home.*

Hope does not disappoint us, and it sometimes points out when we have lacked prudence. I let go of what was already gone. I took hold of my belongings and wits. Then I asked for help.

A police officer told me how to proceed. The parking-lot shuttle driver was sympathetic and dropped me off right beside my car. The lot attendant did him one better: after I paid by check, I asked her for fifteen cents to pay car tolls. She gave me a dollar and best wishes. I drove off into the night, an hour late, many dollars short, light in purse, lighter of heart.

Buddhist teacher and cancer survivor Sandy Boucher says that we can always begin again. Sometimes we have to. I hope to visit Graceland someday.

# PART II

## *Return*

# Ra Chaka

## *Serving time*

After thirty-three years in Illinois prisons, Ra Chaka came out a pretty nice guy.

Of course, he thought he was a pretty nice guy when he went in.

In 1975, Chaka found himself sitting in a county jail on his second armed robbery charge. He was facing an indeterminate sentence that could run up to sixty years and would be no less than twenty. *Why me?* he asked himself. *I don't consider myself a bad person. This gotta be something bigger than me.*

Much to his surprise, he received an answer.

*Why not you? I have prepared you from childhood to go in this direction. You have to serve.*

*Serve?* demanded the prisoner. *Serve what? Whom?*

*Serve people,* came the answer, *like I serve you.*

Now an advocate for people in prison, Chaka can count as preparation for his service to God a harsh and painful childhood. He didn't grow up with a mother or father; his mother died, his father drifted, trying to play music, spending time in jail. As a boy, Chaka was shuffled from one relative to another in the central Illinois towns of Springfield and East St. Louis. One of the relatives he lived with used to beat him with switches that she would first braid together as the boy watched. Another relative ruled her houseful of children by the old-fashioned "southern pecking order," which favored the lightest-skinned children with the closest blood ties. Chaka was dark-skinned, and a distant relative to boot, which assured him a spot low in the order.

"Every time I started battling, I would be in the wrong," Chaka says of trying to fit into different households. Sure, some people occasionally gave him guidance, telling him to stay in school, to study. A few people cared for him the way children are supposed to be cared for. A grandmother tried; Chaka also remembers a woman in a home where he was placed in East St. Louis. She used to help him with his homework and even sent him to a Catholic school, giving him his first introduction to religion.

But doing what you're supposed to do and concentrating on school were not easy for a boy who kept changing where he called home. And so his journey eventually led him to the streets. He was first locked up at age eight; by age ten, he was a resident of the youth detention facility in St. Charles, Illinois.

"I spent thirteen, fourteen months there," Chaka says. "I don't even remember what I done. Probably had to do with stealing." Or, he adds, running away from the different homes where he was supposed to be living. He did that a lot.

"I thought I was escaping abuse, but I was running into harm's way."

Not surprisingly, the road Chaka went down led him directly to jail. By 1975, when he was thirty, he was facing his second prison sentence for armed robbery. This time the sentence was long and uncertain: twenty to sixty years in jail. Illinois law in effect at the time permitted sentencing to an indeterminate term.

That was a long time, and a long time ago. Now, at age fifty-five, Chaka is a solidly built, bespectacled man whose neat beard is sprinkled with gray. I tell him he looks younger. "Prison has a way of preserving some of us," he says with a chuckle. Soft-spoken, Chaka doesn't sound like he spent his formative years on the streets and thirty-plus years in jail amid a population of criminals. I ask him: "Who was the Chaka of twenty-five years ago that pulled a gun on another human being?"

"That was about survival," he says. "It was about accumulating the dollars, pure and simple."

It didn't get him a lot of money, either, but it sure did earn him plenty of prison time. "It was just enough to survive, and seem like every time I would do it, I would get caught," he muses. "That should tell you something."

Definitely adding to his bespectacled respectability is the fat briefcase he hauls around, stuffed with papers and folders, material for the next meeting, the next rally, the next issue, the next case. Chaka could be a lawyer; he certainly knows enough about the law, from working with lawyers as an activist and from years spent in prison law libraries. But the law bars former felons from admission, blocking one high-paying career from guys who usually have a hard time finding employment once they've paid their debt to society.

As director of community affairs for the Prison Action Committee, Chaka talks to audiences of all sorts, and he's got the right job: he is a gifted communicator. When he tells stories about his prison experiences, he can flip into street talk faster than a Chicago minute. Then his language and tone convey the challenges, confrontations, and threats that are the everyday currency of men who have nothing but time to keep simmering whatever tough brew is inside them.

Chaka hands me a few slices of prison life to give me a taste of it.

Once, when working on a fellow prisoner's case, Chaka had to deal with a tough gang enforcer. The man in charge of making photocopies in a prison law library was also a "general": a dangerous and high-ranking member of one of the gangs in prison.

"Ain't getting no copies, man," the general told him. Although Chaka was on his guard, and knew he hadn't exceeded his legal limit of copies—two hundred a month—he recognized that he was facing a different kind of limit here.

"What you mean, man?" he asked.

And back and forth it went, words for survival, tense and terse, until the general eventually understood that Chaka was researching the case of one of his superiors. "Okay, man, you get copies."

"God showed me through that," Chaka concludes. In prison, there are rules about how to get along, and they are unwritten. The whole conversation between the two inmates was about something else altogether: who calls it, who says what goes or doesn't go. In prison, Chaka explains, authorities are nominally in control. In actuality, alliances and affiliations can determine who uses which cell, who gets which job.

"When you are challenged, you got to answer back," says Chaka. "It's the jungle."

Chaka's particular challenge was to remain an independent agent who could move within and between groups in order to do his service time. He read and studied. He read about world religions, law, education. He read the Qur'an and other religious scriptures; he meditated. He got a college degree, and even began studying accounting, was ordained a nondenominational minister by a Christian bishop, and taught law and religion. All these things spread his reputation and earned him freer passage among rival gangs and groups, who would send down the word to take care of their brother, because he was taking care of a brother.

One group, however, didn't particularly warm to his activities.

"I found myself coming in conflict with prison administrations," Chaka explains.

As a jailhouse lawyer, he spent his time listening to prisoners explain their situations. As he listened, he began to hear more, hear deeply, hear inside. It was like looking in a mirror. In helping others, he unexpectedly helped himself.

An inmate "don't tell you just about his case—he dumps," Chaka says. Personal revelation can get messy and involved in prison, when ears to listen are few. "As people began to talk with me, I began to listen to them and I began to see myself. At some point I realized, 'This is why I was running.' But wherever I run to, I carried it with me."

Looking into the eyes of a jailed brother, Chaka saw himself. "I had nightmares," he recalls. "I had dreams. I began to remember conversations—this stuff was coming up. I awakened—that's what happened to me, and I was free."

His name signifies his change. He started life as Bobby Lee Perry, his given name; he gave himself the name Ra Chaka in 1968 and went by it in prison. After he got out, he changed it legally, choosing names that would reflect different parts of his character. *Ra* is the name of the Egyptian god of the sun, representing intuition, or knowing something without having to see it, knowing it with the eye that symbolizes the sun god. "I can see into what things are being said," Ra Chaka says. "That's intuitive."

*Chaka* comes from a nineteenth-century Zulu king and warrior who united factions in his land. "I seen in him a strong character and warrior," the king's namesake explains. "I had to struggle like he struggled."

The change had great spiritual significance for him. "It was more or less a rebirth when I changed my name."

Chaka wasn't released from jail until 1994. By then he had already been working with the Prison Action Committee, formed in 1992 by former offenders (and staffed by them as well). PAC receives foundation and individual support for its operations and its programs, including funding from the United Way of Chicago. It operates a Community Reentry Project to help former offenders come back into their communities, as more than ninety percent of prison inmates eventually do. The program includes GED classes, training in the areas of computer maintenance, tailoring and construction trades, mental-health counseling, assistance with small business ventures and transitional housing. Unless a released inmate has a family to return to, he or she is automatically homeless on the streets, a place where criminal behavior can be an easy habit to slide back into.

PAC has a number of other programs and projects, including one for women who have been sexually abused before entering prison or while in prison. Through correspondence with prisoners, they offer solutions to problems being reported. A Prison Phone Project is gathering information on rates charged prisoners for collect calls. PAC also works with churches and community groups on issues of concern to prisoners' families.

Jim Chapman is a trial lawyer and community activist of many years' standing in Chicago. He was involved in the formation of PAC and has known Chaka even longer, since 1987. The two met when Chaka, then in Pontiac, a maximum-security prison, contacted Jim, who was doing work that brought him into prisons. Chaka wanted help starting a group for men in prison that would promote positive behavior and ready them for returning to the community.

"I can assure you it was all exceptionally positive," says Jim. But prison authorities didn't think so and dispersed the group. Chaka was then transferred to Menard, another maximum-security prison, and the two men stayed in touch.

One day in 1994 Jim's phone rang. "I got a call from this little voice," recalls Jim. "'I'm here, they just let me out.'" Jim was surprised, given the indeterminacy of Chaka's prison term. But Chaka was finally free, and he was ready to work.

"He immediately started working with PAC," Jim recalls. "He just never skipped a beat."

Chaka works on prison reform in Illinois, but he also travels the country in that cause. I met him in New Orleans, where he was a panelist at a national conference on forgiveness and transformation.

In two decades of working with prisoners and former prisoners, Jim has known many. Chaka, however, is most exceptional. "Of all the prisoners coming out of prison, Chaka is probably the most dedicated to a vision that is based on sharing and giving and really trying to change matters," says Jim, who presently serves as president of PAC's board. "He's not as centered as he might think; he has anger, but it's righteous anger."

"Chaka," Jim repeats, "has never skipped a beat."

Chaka says that prison has changed since his experience of it. As if trading in for a new and improved car, our society has

traded in the uncertain hope of slow rehabilitation for the shiny
political promise to get tough on crime. Chaka likes to point
out that the Illinois law that gives the Department of
Corrections its authority doesn't authorize the state to punish
someone. "They're supposed to be there to help," he argues. He
summarizes the now-prevailing ethic he says he once heard
from the lips of a high-ranking prison official: "Crush those
gangbanging punks."

Even as vindictive punishment becomes an acceptable, and
electable, American attitude, the prison industry becomes a
growing part of the American economy. Inmates and their cus-
todians require goods and services. In Illinois alone, more than
44,000 adults are in 37 prisons in the state, watched over by a
little less than 10,000 people working as security and staff.
Throw in every other state, and you have a prison population of
1.3 million people at the beginning of a new millennium.
That's a sixfold increase in the prison census since 1970. It's a
seventy-two percent increase over a decade. However you
interpret the numbers, each one marks a head, and the head
count is exponentially growing.

As costs escalate for this public service, taxpayers get a bill
for toughness on crime. The Illinois Department of
Corrections budget for fiscal year 2000—the budget of one
state alone—exceeds a billion dollars. And wherever there's a
growth industry, there are ways for some to make money.
Companies that manage or service aspects of the prison industry are traded on Wall Street, making the incarceration of more
than one million Americans—usually poor, often unemployed,
largely without high school diplomas and overwhelmingly
black—an activity that is expected to generate a profit for
stockholders. From inmate numbers to security technology,
from food to nonlethal means of behavior control, prison is an
investment that will return.

"It's about money now," says Chaka. "It's good business."

People like Chaka and Jim Chapman and others interested in the human and social costs of incarcerating a generation say that change will have to take place at the front end, in communities where crime can be prevented through a host of means, from greater love for one's neighbor to the assurance of a living wage and affordable and decent housing.

Having served his prison time, Chaka now serves his community, his city, his brothers and sisters. He has a daughter, too, but father and daughter are estranged. She was raised by an aunt. Chaka hopes that might change someday.

"She blamed me for the life I led," he says. "I tried to explain about [my] not having a mother or father, about being shipped through juvenile facilities, but it hasn't been her experience—and I understand that now myself."

Although he can't re-raise his own child, Chaka can concern himself with other people's children. He frequently talks to school audiences; he sees stuff; kids come to him and tell him about how hard they have it. When they tell him, "You can't understand," he says, "I went through the same kind of stuff thirty, forty years ago."

It's taken time, pain, mistakes, consequences, but Chaka has a key now that will keep him from getting locked up, that will keep him free.

"If there is such a place as heaven, it'll be for the person who done the most work on behalf of somebody else," Chaka muses. "That is the only price you have to pay to get in. That's what Jesus said, that's your key to the kingdom."

# Melody Green
*Still water*

*And early in the morning he came walking toward them on the sea.*

—Matthew 14:25

Melody Green has a job at sea now, and it's a good place to think about things. Out there—when the water is still and featureless, stretching for miles and miles—things seem a little simpler, a lot vaster. The waters of the Gulf of Mexico are like a fresh sheet of paper on which she can write a new story. And she's certainly trying to do just that.

Her old story was not a happy one. It was about years of drug addiction, years of rebellion and anger. Naturally, that story starts with a child: herself, scared and shy. She had good reason. Life with an alcoholic father was chaotic, until one climactic day when he left the family picture.

The men closest to her when she was young taught Melody a pattern: express anger through abuse, either physical or verbal. She didn't learn many ways, though, of expressing love.

"What I thought was love was abuse," she says, as she looks back now from her new perspective.

Although she was just a child, and children are pretty helpless when grown-ups prey on them, Melody managed to figure out a couple of ways to escape. She'd stay in her room—and stay there and stay there. It was safe there. Nice day out? So what?

"I was a kid that stayed in my room," she says. "I had to be forced to go out to play."

When Melody couldn't stay inside her room, she'd stay inside herself. Wouldn't talk, wouldn't say what was wrong or even what was what. She was shy, withdrawn. "You know how kids play?" she asks, as she describes her childhood. "I didn't do that."

In fact, Melody hardly has any specific memories of her childhood, but one sticks out in a vivid, fragmented way, like a bad dream. She remembers when her father left. He and her mother were having a big fight. There was also a bat—a baseball bat—and somebody was swinging it. Her father was hurt.

"I can't picture his face," Melody says today, trying to remember what her father looked like. "There was a lot of blood, and that was the last time I remember seeing him." After that, her father was gone. She doesn't remember how old she was—or exactly when her stepfather entered the family.

"I have no memories of anything but that," she says. "I was a sad kid."

But Melody couldn't stay in her room and within her own silence forever. At age thirteen, she was introduced to something that allowed her an exit door from whatever place she had to be. She could use drugs.

And that's what she did. Instead of being present in high school to learn, her body was there, but her mind was somewhere else, wherever the drugs could take her. She didn't finish school. It wasn't because there are bad public schools in

New Orleans, shes admits, where she was born and raised. She doesn't blame the schools. "I can't say it was no-good schools. I just wasn't there."

Melody had already learned that love wasn't reliable or especially kindly. Now, though, she had something to help her cope with problems as they arose: drugs. "Anything that happened, I'd want to get loaded."

But there were things in her life that would moderate that craving for a high. As time went on, Melody had children, three of them. Each time, they provided deliverance from drugs, as she managed to stay off drugs and alcohol during each pregnancy. She knew she didn't want, or couldn't handle, tiny, damaged babies, like addicted friends of hers were having to do. Each time, her children brought her new opportunities to learn to be a parent. Given her own upbringing, however, she brought belligerence to the task of raising children. The children wouldn't do what she'd say, so she'd threaten to "whup 'em"—frustrated, hollering, and ineffective. "I was that parent," she acknowledges, shaking her head.

But Melody's children were a lifeline as well as teachers of parenting. Maybe it was maternal instinct; maybe it was the secret presence within. Despite her addiction, she managed to keep decent jobs, hiding her relationship with drugs well enough to function and pay the bills. Maybe it was her skill at living behind a mask of quiet that made her so good at fooling people. She actually fooled her own mother.

"I didn't know you were that bad," her mother told her later, when drug addiction was no longer calling the shots in Melody's life.

During the addiction years, Melody realized small opportunities opening up for her. One job she especially remembers for the experience it opened to her. She worked with disabled people as an aide, and had a rewarding relationship with a client with cerebral palsy. Melody was the only one who could understand the impaired speech of her client, and she understood it well, much to everyone's amazement. "I understood her like I understand what you're saying," she explains to me. "I don't know how. I just believe that God put me in her life." Or perhaps what actually happened is that God put this woman into Melody's life.

Does God find the lost or do they stumble over what has always been there? This is how Melody found her answer to that question, after getting some hints along the way. "It happened in my own experience," she says.

Every addict vividly remembers the bottom. For Melody, it was in 1992. "I remember walking down the street, crying unmercifully," she recalls, "and I said, 'Please help me.' I ended up in an emergency room. I sat in the corner for two hours and nobody came. Finally, somebody grabbed me by the arm."

In the hospital, Melody was finally admitted into a drug treatment program—even though she didn't know she needed it, didn't know to ask for it. She doesn't know who grabbed her by the arm, but she was led—as much by God answering her cry for help as by hospital personnel diagnosing her situation and prescribing a treatment program.

Melody had to let herself be led, though. "I've always been a rebellious person," she explains, her tone of voice growing loud, bringing out just exactly what this big-boned, heavy woman means. "You ain't gonna tell me what to do."

But when Melody finally found a God who would not punish her and send her straight to damnation, as the God of her Baptist-church childhood was always threatening to do, she became more willing to listen. As is the case for many addicts, she found her merciful God through a 12-Step Program. This God promised help rather than hell and, over time, she became willing to let go of her drug addiction. "When I allowed God to work, it worked," she adds. She has been clean—drug free—for more than five years.

It wasn't easy; after all, addiction is a powerful opponent who can get up from the mat and deliver more blows. The first time Melody tried getting clean, she had a relapse after three years, and that hurt her kids, she says. They were confused, because they thought the addiction was over and didn't understand just how powerful and insidious the lure of drugs could be.

"I think everything I go through is a test," she says. "There's struggles and struggles. But," she adds, "if we don't go through new struggles, we don't have any experience."

Eventually Melody's path led to Project Return, an innovative program at Tulane University Medical Center designed to help men and women released from prison successfully return to their neighborhoods. A hidden and intractable social cancer, recidivism—return to prison for those who have been there—is shockingly high. Various studies of groups of former offenders show that, at a minimum, half of them return to prison for another offense. Because virtually everyone who goes to jail eventually gets out, a vicious cycle can begin for former offenders as well as the communities to which they return.

Started in 1993, Project Return intends to short-circuit this cycle of crime and punishment that costs society, crime victims, and crime perpetrators. The project offers a ninety-day, full-time program of education, addiction treatment, job training, and counseling, working in concert on the four areas of skills and knowledge in which former prisoners invariably need to do catch-up work. A peer-group program follows a model developed by M. Scott Peck for community building. This part of the project teaches conflict resolution and self-awareness.

Results from Project Return have been promising enough to win funding support from the New Orleans business community. In 2000, a research report by the city's Metropolitan

Crime Commission to measure recidivism concluded that the program is effective, cutting in half recidivism among those who complete the program after four years.

A stint Melody did in jail qualified her for the program. As she tells it, she got in an argument with a close friend over a car in 1991. She shoved her friend, resulting in an arrest for battery. She went to jail, paid a fine, and thought the chapter was closed until a warrant for her arrest was issued in 1999, based, she says, on bad record-keeping in the justice system.

Thus, in spring 2000, Melody was led to Project Return by another recovering drug addict who was a project graduate. Her incarceration was finally a positive thing: because of it, she could enter the program.

At Project Return, Melody began working on her GED, trying to make good on the education she forfeited in her teen years. Rochelle Perry, one of her teachers at Project Return, was confident that her student had what it takes to succeed. Melody has the "want-to," says Rochelle, who is also Project Return's Assistant Director of Operations, pointing out that Melody has a willing spirit—and motivation is half the effort. "She has the desire. She's faced her ghosts and her demons, but she is going to walk a new path despite their presence."

Through the project, Melody also secured a good-paying job working as a galley hand on an offshore oil rig. Being out in the middle of the Gulf of Mexico—it takes an hour and forty-five minutes by helicopter to get there—is like being anywhere or nowhere. Nighttime in the middle of the featureless waters, like the waters at creation's beginning, is a time for filling in the blanks. "There's nothing you can see," Melody says. "It's pitch dark, dark, dark."

One night out there on the Gulf, Melody opened the door of the kitchen to look out across the waters. It was at the end of sunset, when only a tiny edge of daylight is left at the horizon, when all is uniform darkness except for a slim stream of light at the seam of heaven and earth. Melody looked at the splendor and was grateful for simple beauty, deep change, and the work of God, there on the waters, in her line of sight, there in her very own experience.

"And," she adds with a practical laugh, "it didn't cost me nothin'."

Through Project Return Melody made a lot of friends. The girl who used to stay in her room and not say anything to anybody when she was a young child is now a friendly woman, hello-ing and bear-hugging and nodding to person after person walking by as she and I talk outside a Project Return conference where we have met.

Afterward, Melody and I have lunch and she introduces me to a friend, Darlene Lewis. A short woman, Darlene has on a square-shouldered business suit and dark-rimmed glasses, and her hair is close-cropped and neat. She looks like the accountant she is, tailored and organized. Darlene helps Melody get organized; the two joke that she is Melody's secretary. Melody could use a secretary, because her offshore-rig job keeps her incommunicado from routine matters for weeks at a time, until it's time for "shore leave." She works twelve hours a day, seven days a week, for two, three, sometimes four weeks, depending on the shift she's assigned. She then has a week or two off. It's a wearying schedule.

Melody's best friend, Alice County, has been with her through very thick and very thin, trying times, back in the addiction years, when Melody would let domestic things slide and Alice would step in to keep things going. Following the 12 Steps, Melody has made her amends to her friend. "A person can still love me the same, no matter what," is how Melody now gratefully puts it. She tells me specially about this; affirming her friend's abiding and unconditioned care is important.

Melody's needs now are fairly practical: she could use affordable health care. Health insurance will kick in at her new job but, in the meantime, she is paying cash for the medicine she needs to control hypertension. Her doctor is experimenting to see which medication will be most effective, and sometimes she feels side effects: one of them is being cash-short after paying for very expensive drugs.

Melody's three children are mostly grown now and, at age forty-three she is already a grandmother of two. Her oldest daughter, twenty-two, has two children, ages two and five, and the grandchildren's antics are a source of entertainment and joy. Melody's son is twenty, and her youngest, a daughter, is nineteen. If life sends tests—her children inherited Melody's rebelliousness—it also sends renewal, in the form of grandchildren. And it sends feedback to let Melody know that her faith is worth it.

"If I've changed this much," she says, "I know it can be done, because it has been done."

Melody also has ambitions for further schooling, once she obtains her GED. She's interested in working as a substance-abuse counselor with teenagers. It's been "on my heart," she says. It's tantalizing that she might be able to set future Melodys on the right track much earlier and with less pain.

Developing a deeper relationship with God also beckons. Although Melody's searching for the right place to go, she's not yet churchgoing. "That's been sort of a struggle for me because I still have this thing—that churches are a bunch of bullcrap," she says, choosing an expletive that will honor her vow to clean up her language. But she knows there's a place out there where she can converse comfortably with the God who accepts her. "I just have to keep looking," she says. "God loves me no matter what. I don't have to be a certain way for him to love me."

Melody used to think that God must not be very powerful or very effective, with all the suffering, hunger, and pain in the world. But if there's suffering, there is also mercy. And Melody knows, from looking at her own life, the freeing power of change, the power to begin anew. Out there on the dark waters, in the Gulf, she has time to think about God and the next steps along the journey of her life. Wounds can heal. Pain can stop. Prayer provides relief. The sun goes down in the Gulf of Mexico and rises again, the same sun on a brand new day, when things can look so different. And the legacy of childhood, stored inside like a box once wrapped in sadness, becomes a beautiful gift.

"The abuse part," says Melody, "is changing into the love part."

"Changing," she clarifies with a deep laugh. "I'm working on it."

Melody is not shy about sharing her story, hoping that people can learn something from the path she has walked. From different groups she has been in, she has learned the value of telling her tale to others. But she can't help being surprised that anyone would be interested in an everyday redemption like hers. She's been thinking about that, too, when the sun goes down and the dark comes up and she's out there on the big water with nothing except her thoughts between her and God's horizon. "I wonder," she says slowly. "That's something: that someone is interested in my story."

# Postcard

## *New Orleans*

It's hot here even though it's October. The locals say it's always hot here. Second-floor balconies wrapping around this city's antebellum houses drip the foliage of ferns and other delicate vining houseplants, like jungle grace notes.

I was here thirty years ago, when I was a teenager in love. Some things haven't changed. The French Quarter is still home to the same famous restaurants from the nineteenth century: The Court of the Two Sisters, Galatoire's, Antoine's. I read the menu from Antoine's posted in the window: oysters Rockefeller and other expensive dishes. Who's eating in there, I wonder.

My stop is the celebrated and more affordable Café du Monde, also in the French Quarter, where a customer can walk in, grab a vacant seat, and order a café au lait and three beignets, snowy with powdered sugar and fresh from the deep fryer. The staff wear green-and-white paper caps that are part of their uniform, and the limited menu is posted on the napkin containers sitting on each table. The tables here are so tiny, a girl and her boyfriend could easily meet knees under the table and eyes over it. Thirty years later, though, I'm more conscious of families crowded around tables than teenage lovers drinking coffee and each other's company.

I had to come here again because I remember the coffee and its bitter taste—coffee tamed with chicory, made strong and diluted with hot milk, different tastes on the tongue, married yet distinct. It feels like a European cafe, with the little tables, historic buildings wherever you look, the world strolling by, its pace of life as leisurely as the speed of this city's lumbering streetcars.

The Café du Monde looks onto Jackson Square, which is surrounded by a pedestrian mall filled mostly with palm readers at tables and artists displaying their wares on the black iron fence surrounding the square. The square abuts St. Louis Cathedral, an 1850 structure that deliberately calls to mind Europe's great houses of God.

History has been made here. Plaques on the quarter's oldest buildings remind visitors that this place was once Spanish, then it was French, throw in African influence throughout and *voilà*: heritage gumbo.

This exotic place got folded into my own personal history, like a hint of chicory in the cup of weak coffee you drink with your supper if you're a Pole from Chicago. In New Orleans—which revels in its reputation as "The Big Easy" with a wink and a nod and lots of beer flowing on Bourbon Street—I got a food education and other lessons.

## *1970*

I was a Polish American girl from Chicago visiting my boyfriend in 1970. Raised in a working-class family, I'd never seen an artichoke in person. So I got a lesson in how to eat artichokes: dip the steamed leaves in melted butter and draw them deliberately through your teeth. I was also introduced to crawfish, even though I never actually consumed one because I couldn't bring myself to suck their brains out. "Head's the best part," they kept telling seventeen-year-old me to broaden my knowledge of cuisine and double entendre.

My boyfriend's name was Tommy, and his last name was *très* French. He gave me a silver and turquoise ring that I still wear thirty years later. I put it on one day and never took it off. It's as if it had become part of my finger, much the same way Tommy became part of my life, still there but no longer noticeable, the way history is when it has been formative but is now forgotten—like the Spanish influence in New Orleans, still there, the finger of the past poking the shifting, alive present.

I remember exotic, delicious food: eggs sardou, brown sugar pralines—buttery and melting sweet in the mouth. I remember myself at age seventeen, hundreds of miles from home, wondering how in heaven I ever badgered my mother into allowing her teenager to travel economy mode on a Greyhound bus to New Orleans to visit her boyfriend, even if they did like him because he was very, very polite and respectful.

Respectful: naturally she didn't know about those passionate kisses from a French boy from New Orleans. I still wear the ring, I still remember the time we steamed up the windows of his Volkswagen, but perhaps it was the humid Louisiana night, filled with bright stars and big, easy kisses and bone-invasive damp.

Mom liked Tommy, but she wasn't ready when I told her—home in 1973 during a college vacation—that I was no longer a virgin. She didn't ask who, so I spared her the revelation that it wasn't even Tommy, but someone else.

When I saw Mom's reaction, though, I was stricken. Guilt found me at night, in the dark, and began nibbling, like a mouse stowed on board ship, at my emotional keel. At age nineteen, away at college shortly after this conversation with my mother, I became unable to sleep.

I was then living with my boyfriend, yet another truth I didn't dare tell my mother, much as I longed for the ability to confide in her. I began having bad dreams, nightmares that would frighten me out of sleep. Tearing away the blinders of sleep, I would fight my way out of a dreamworld peopled with shadows, intruders, assailants, out to harm me.

I deduced a logical solution to this dream-danger. Judgment and punishment awaited me if I closed my eyes; therefore, I would not sleep. For nearly six weeks, a friend would often stay awake with me. Marsha had a low, soothing voice. As college students do, we would talk intensely, lamplight keeping the dark at bay and brightening our enthusiastic ideas until wee hours, when I was so exhausted that my defenses against sleep's attack crumbled, and I fell into it. But I felt I had a sentinel there in my friend.

Over weeks, the grip of guilt loosened and, eventually, I no longer needed an escort to dreamland. I filed away this episode as another little oddity. After all, didn't everybody flip out every so often? So it seemed by the pattern of my father, whose emotional torment recurred at intervals we knew would come, but never knew just when.

Thirty years later, as soon as I am inside my hotel room in the Garden District, I unload my bags. The air's a little close; it's hot in the room and the air conditioner is old and hard to adjust to the right degree of cool.

I'm on a mission. I open every drawer. There's the Bible in a hotel room in this alcohol- and religion-soaked city, and in the very last drawer is the phone book. I riffle the pages to B to locate that French last name of his. There are six columns' worth, just as there would be six columns if he were to look up

Nelson in a northern-city phone book. There are five listings of Tommy B; is he one of them?

Can't find out unless I dial.

I'm looking for a Tom B who grew up in Metairie, I say, stumbling over words to Tom B number 1. Where did you grow up? I await his answer, my heart pitty-thumping, wondering what I'll say if he answers "yes."

Chalmette, he says. Thud goes my heart and I start breathing normally again and saying, "Wrong number, excuse me"—and I redial. I redial and redial, not finding my Tom B, but hope springing eternal in my foolish heart. I'm looking for the boy who is now a man who could be anywhere in the United States, and I imagine that he's grown older but gone nowhere, like me, changed but stayed the same somehow, no longer Tommy but Tom yet still in suburban New Orleans, proceeding on his own journey. Me, I am the girl I was but also different; some things change, some stay the same. I learned that in high school French class: *plus ça change, plus ça reste*.

It's hard to sleep—must be revenge of the chicory coffee. My mind is riffling through a few pages of personal history and re-understanding. Beginning again does not mean shedding the past or denying it; it means shouldering it with acceptance. Acceptance provides the strength to carry and to carry on.

I think of Melody Green, my teacher on this visit to New Orleans, like and unlike previous trips. Sustain in me a willing spirit, the psalmist prays; Melody has the want-to, her teacher says.

The psalmist says more in Psalm 51, a good one for the recycled:

> The sacrifice acceptable to God is a broken spirit;
>> a broken and contrite heart, O God,
>>> you will not despise (Psalm 51:17).

Sustain in me and sustain me.

And sinners will return to you (Psalm 51:13).

They will return.

# PART III

*Revision*

# Jorge Valdés
## *Swept clean*

> *Purge me with hyssop, and I shall be clean;*
>   *wash me, and I shall be whiter*
>     *than snow.*

—Psalm 51:7

Jorge Valdés should be dead. He lived through a plane crash. Torture in a Panamanian jail. Ten years in prison. An attempted hit on his life killed an associate instead.

Jorge Valdés should be rich. He used to be. He owned a ranch full of horses and a garage full of Porsches. He had women, penthouses, Rolexes, bodyguards, millions of dollars, power. He had everything the good life had to offer, one for each day of the week, in different colors.

"Man," Jorge says, his Cuban origin apparent in his accent even after thirty-five years in America, "I was miserable."

"'For what will it profit them if they gain the whole world but forfeit their life?'" (Matthew 16:26)

Jorge Valdés was a criminal, bringing tons of cocaine into the United States in the late 1970s, telling himself he was only selling people—responsible adults—what they wanted. He was the drug-running Medellin cartel's man in the U.S., doing business for them. He was a businessman, in it for the money.

Never mind the corruption of officials in several countries, one key to permitting drug trade to continue and confound law enforcement. Never mind the small-fries down the distribution chain, tearing apart and bankrupting their families with legal woes and bills once they were arrested. And never mind the children of users: crack babies who tremble and cry and will not be soothed.

"I look back now," he says. "How could I be so hard?"

Jorge spent ten years in jail, serving time in two federal prisons, sentenced twice for bringing drugs into the United States. The second time was a little different, though. He pled guilty to charges that could have earned him eight life sentences in jail. He wanted to come clean with himself, God, and the government.

From the government he got ten years. From God he got new direction.

Jorge, now an ex-felon, is director of Coming Clean Ministries in suburban Atlanta and himself a father of five children. "I'm glad that my sinful past does not bind me," he says. But while mercy is his, so are the consequences of what he has done, ready to remind him in unexpected encounters. "Every crime, everything we do has a reaction to it."

The crack babies haunt Jorge most. He sees them when he is asked to join in prayer for them. He hears about them—a baby born in the toilet of a crack house, saved from death because the toilet didn't flush. They stay with him, as does the memory of his own little girl, Krystle, crying for him in the night outside his bedroom door while he was inside the room with a couple of women.

This is how Jorge tells it when he talks to kids and tells them not to do what he's done. "I told people, 'I'm gonna die a gangster.' We tell ourselves so many lies that eventually we believe those lies," he says to a group of one hundred people, including teens, gathered in an Aurora, Illinois, youth recreation center. "There was nothing on God's earth I didn't have twice."

Jorge couldn't make up his mind what color Corvette to buy, so he bought three. He rented a penthouse apartment in New York that cost him $20,000 a month, and he stayed there only four times. He went out with beautiful women, and ended up hating them. Nothing he could buy made him happy. He likes to point this out to his audiences, kids, who are dressed in Nikes, baggy red-white-and-denim-blue Tommy Hilfiger clothes, and other gotta-have labels. They're listening to a guy who had what they think they want.

Jorge started modestly. A refugee with his family from Castro's Cuba in 1966, he turned out to be pretty precocious with numbers. He studied accounting, worked for the Federal Reserve Bank at age seventeen, and started meeting older businessmen and beautiful women. The businessmen impressed him—and he wanted to impress the women. Before long, his tastes, talents, and ambitions gained him the company of dishonest associates, and he became involved in money laundering and forming business "fronts" to move money into his pockets and the pockets of others. Eventually, his international business connections hooked him up with people whose business interest was cocaine. With that drug gaining popularity in the '70s, Jorge saw drug-running as the perfect business opportunity. It was 1977, and he was twenty-one years old.

Jorge flew back and forth between Miami and Chicago, to Bolivia and Colombia, transporting drugs, making connections, even watching cocaine being processed. His business was lucrative, but not for long. By early 1979, trouble with a Bolivian connection required his presence. The return flight was fateful: the plane carrying Jorge, three other men, and $4.5 million in cocaine crashed in Panama, plunging Jorge into a nightmare of torture and political corruption that ended when he was freed from a Panamanian jail and promptly steered back to American soil—and arrested.

Jorge ended up with a sentence of fifteen years, but that wasn't enough to deter him from continuing a drug operation even while in prison. When he was paroled in 1984, he went back to the drug business, got married, had children, watched drug associates die, and had a heart attack at age thirty-one. His life changed slowly, divorce and depression weighing on him. By 1990, he had stopped selling drugs, was remarried, making money legitimately as a horse breeder, and beginning to know God.

Then Jorge was arrested again on conspiracy charges related to his previous activities and associates. Facing the possibility of eight life sentences, Jorge decided to plead guilty in order to come clean with God and the state. He also agreed to forfeit $15 million in assets to the government, leaving him with nothing but one horse named Heaven Sent. He was baptized in jail in Mobile County, Alabama. Two federal drug agents who built the case against him testified at his sentencing hearing that he had changed. He was sentenced to ten years.

While serving his sentence in a federal prison in Georgia, he completed a bachelor's degree from Southeastern Bible College, then, with fine spiritual irony, earned a master's degree in theology in 1996 from Wheaton College, alma mater of Billy Graham. When early release from prison freed him to pursue more studies, he went on to attain a doctorate in New Testament studies from Loyola University in Chicago in 1999.

Jorge's life sounds like a movie; in fact, he says there has been interest in making one. His book *Coming Clean* was published in 1999, and it reads like an airport-rack suspense novel:

the life of a drug kingpin with international high rollers, drugs, political corruption, violence, courtroom drama. If a movie gets made, he doesn't want it to be so secular that it glorifies his former lifestyle, but he doesn't want it to be an "unreal Christian" script, either. "It's done in [God's] timing, I guess," he says.

When I meet Jorge in my hometown of Aurora, an ex-blue-collar city filled with shuttered factories, 110 houses of worship, and the opportunities and tensions of cultural and racial diversity, he has come to talk to youth. He is also a keynote speaker for Wayside Cross Ministries, an Aurora evangelical Christian organization that offers rehabilitation programs for addicted men and women and runs a long-standing ministry at the county jail, where other potential Jorges are spending time.

Inside a drafty coffeehouse set within an old local church, underneath electric chandeliers suspended from high ceilings, the former multimillion-dollar drug kingpin is sitting at a tiny glass-topped table that may have been recycled from some ice cream shop. He's chatting with a group of pastors who are T-shirted, greened-up for St. Patrick's Day, or otherwise casually dressed. Jorge is wearing a Tommy Hilfiger green-and-white-striped polo shirt.

"We have so many suburban kids committing suicide," he says. "Sin has jumped the white picket fence and is knocking at the door."

Not surprisingly, Jorge is highly opinionated about the scope of drugs in the culture, since he knows firsthand how the drug economy works. "As long as America is the most addicted country in the world, we can't clean up Colombia," he tells the pastors. "There's too much money. The corruption is immense."

When Jorge's cellular phone rings, he excuses himself. "My wife," he explains, taking the call and speaking quietly to her in English and Spanish. He met his wife, Sujey, a woman from

Medellin, Colombia, at Wheaton College in 1996, when he was tutoring her in Greek. The couple has a young son, born in 1999. Jorge's oldest child is twenty-two.

"I'm starting over," Jorge the father explains with a smile.

Although Jorge travels around the country with his ministry to speak to youth, in divine irony, he also helps his wife with a housecleaning business she operates to pay the bills. This gives Jorge an opportunity to minister to people informally as well. "What else can I do but this?" he asks with a shrug.

On a platform, Jorge is pretty down to earth, speaking not about doctrine but his own lived and remembered experience. From his experience he can tell young people that sin has a price. From his experience he can demonstrate that crime doesn't pay, however it might appear momentarily to the contrary. From his experience he can say that the spiritual journey can replace the criminal spree.

"God called me to do this," he explains to his audience. African American, Caucasian, Hispanic teens lean forward to listen. "My agenda is to see you make a difference in your community and your world."

Jorge remembers his inner struggle when authorities confiscated his assets, even as he had been negotiating to turn them over voluntarily. He was in jail, stripped of freedom, permanently deprived of millions of dollars of material possessions. He quelled his anger; he also quelled a sense of worthlessness, finding power and real value in his new relationship with a forgiving God.

"In this county jail, without nothing, my life meant something," he says. "For the first time in my life I knew I meant something. Sin is fun, but I gotta tell you something: it's got a hell of a price."

Some of the kids who hear Jorge's message wear jeans and baggy garb. Some are students who have come over from

Wheaton College, Jorge's alma mater. Some are local teens who use God's Gym, a recreation facility that offers teens a faith-based alternative to hanging out on street corners. Still others know something about Jorge's path through experience.

"God is never tired of second beginnings," says Eddie Wells, a graduate of Koinonia House, which helps former prisoners reenter the community after they leave jail. "It really gives you hope."

Manny Mill, founder of Koinonia House, is also Jorge's mentor. Manny first came into contact with Jorge when Jorge wrote him from prison. The two had a lot in common: both are from Cuba, both are Wheaton grads, and both spent time in federal prison. Manny served a little less than two years for forgery. Although he first wanted to become a prison chaplain, his vision changed, and he began Koinonia House in Wheaton, Illinois, in 1991.

The two men did not actually meet until Jorge came to Wheaton to finish his studies. Manny attended Jorge's wedding, advises him in his ministry, and talks with him once a week. Now Jorge is on the board of Manny's own organization.

"He's come a long way," says Manny of his mentee. "He's been very much faithful to his faith."

Around Christmastime I check back with Jorge, who lives in suburban Atlanta. He tells me he's continued to speak around the country, and shared a bill in the fall with Clinton special prosecutor Kenneth Starr. Both were featured speakers at the annual national convention of Concerned Women of America, a conservative women's public-policy group. He has done a short teaching stint on Hispanic theology at Wheaton College. He has an outline for a new book, on the experiences, perils, and possibilities of staying clean. For those who have spent time in jail, going back is statistically likely.

"Coming clean is still a lot easier than other things afterward," Jorge says. His rehabilitation was made easier by having a family and an education—two factors that help former offenders succeed in returning to their communities.

Jorge also has plans for continuing his work with youth, backed by like-minded public and business figures he's beginning to work with. And he has heard from someone working in the jails of Panama that his written account of his experience has made a difference to some prisoners there now, twenty years later. And his wife's cleaning business continues to grow and he continues to help. "I'm doing a lot of that with her," Jorge says. "It keeps me humble."

As you would expect from someone with a Ph.D. in New Testament studies, Jorge is ready with citations from the Bible. He signs my copy of his book with this reference:

> So if anyone is in Christ, there is a new creation: everything old has passed away; see, everything has become new! (2 Corinthians 5:17)

# Liz Curtis Higgs
*Good-news humor*

> *He will wipe every tear from their eyes.*
> —Revelation 21:4

Like a stand-up comic prowling in the club spotlight, Liz Curtis Higgs works the crowd. The former radio personality commands the stage with ease, using elastic face, trained radio-professional voice, and ample body to get her audience laughing.

Liz's life as a funny lady started when she was a child, of course. "In my family," she explains, "you had to be funny or you were asked to leave."

The folks gathered in the auditorium-like sanctuary at First Church of the Nazarene, Indianapolis, are hooting—their laughter pealing like happy church bells in a usually solemn space. Liz keeps firing the one-liners, tickling everyone's jovial button and loosening up the men in their sport coats and the women in their Sunday-church clothes—because even though it's Friday, they're in church in Indianapolis. Liz makes fun of middle age ("God gives you more to laugh about"); of her own experiences, like having an eleven-pound baby ("Why have a baby when you can have a toddler?"); the stodginess too frequently found in churches ("So often the church looks like a pickle, miserable and sour").

Laughter is salvation; underneath the smile, Liz is serious about its value for spiritual health. Psychologists say humor is a mature defense; Liz says at one point in her routine that comedy is tragedy plus time. Laughter—a merry heart—doeth good, the Bible says, a passage Liz likes to cite.

Liz has brought her good humor to the annual district women's conference for the Nazarene churches. She does only three dozen of these engagements a year, having cut down from the hundred she used to do. She needs more time to write; the most recent of her fifteen books—she published two in 1999 and two in 2000—are best-sellers and more are in the works. Time with her family is important, too; she is so organized that "F" on her calendar stands for "family time." On "W"—writing—days, she holes up in her phone-less writing loft at Laughing Heart Farm in Louisville, Kentucky, and tells her son and daughter how to get her attention in the event of an emergency. "I tell them that if they need me, take the garden hose and squirt the window," she says. They do it often, she adds.

Liz's speech is as full of gags as her life is now full of gigs, kids, and books. The road that led her out of a childhood in the idyllic small town of Lititz, Pennsylvania, has brought her a measure of fame in the world of evangelical Christians, especially among women. It was not a destination she would have anticipated twenty years ago, however, when her road was most likely to lead to the next bar or the next guy. Southern Comfort, that sweet amber-colored liquor that sticks to shot glass and tongue, was her drink of choice, pot the drug, and the guy—well, any mildly interested one would do.

Before she wrote *Bad Girls of the Bible* and *Really Bad Girls of the Bible*, Liz wrote the book on being a bad girl. It wasn't much of a reach to do the books of fictional retellings of "bad" women depicted in the Bible; Liz simply had to remember how lost she had once been and what she found out through her own mistakes. She likes to tell people that the morally notorious radio personality Howard Stern, a colleague in her disc-jockey days in the late '70s in Detroit, once counseled her to clean up her act. She spares the details, but uses a little bit of autobiographical material in the prefaces to the *Bad Girls* books to establish her credentials.

She finally did clean up her act in 1982, when she was working on radio in Louisville and had come under the influence not of alcohol or drugs, but a pair of friends and colleagues with whom she had started going to church. One Sunday morning in February, singing "I Have Decided to Follow Jesus" in the choir, Liz made the decision to sign up in the ranks of followers, surprising everybody—herself included.

Her decision wasn't completely out of the blue, however. She had been letting the sermons of previous Sundays creep into her consciousness, albeit slowly. That the Bible had something to say to her and that Jesus was the ultimate guy who loved her began dawning on her as realities. She had already met with the church pastor—still her pastor today, nearly twenty years later. He acknowledged what she had told him about herself by telling her merely that she was leading a "worldly" life.

Liz was heartened by her pastor's response. *Worldly* sounded like he understood her without requiring her to write her deeds in detail on God's blackboard. "Oh, good," she thought, "I don't have to confess every separate little thing." And so she made her decision public, and began Bible study in earnest—with the woman who became her "foster mother": Doris "Doc" Foster, another member of her church in Louisville. "[Liz] was a single lady just coming to know the Lord and she had four hundred questions," recalls Doc. "I had this chocolate cake that she dearly loved—a Texas chocolate cake—and she would check the top of the microwave and say, 'Yeah, I'll stay for supper.'"

"Lizzie was deep," adds her mentor in a friendly, set-a-spell Kentucky accent, "before she even knew what she was talking about. You could see the potential in her in so many ways."

Liz's new faith walk was a little wobbly at first, but slowly and steadily it led her in new spiritual and professional directions. As a radio personality, she had always had an unseen audience. Then she began speaking in public, where she was no longer a disembodied voice—indeed, she was amply embodied—and reaction from her hearers was inescapable and immediate.

Liz was initially afraid to tell her own story of finding faith, but remembers the day she did it for the first time. It was later in 1982, just ten months after she had made her faith commitment, and she spoke in her own church. "I spoke for five minutes, and they laughed and they cried and my pastor said, 'Liz, I think you've found your calling.'"

And he was right. Changes began multiplying in Liz's life. In 1985 she met Bill Higgs, a minister, computer guy, and Ph.D. in Hebrew, and they married the following year. In 1986 she was ready to leave a full-time, high-paying job in radio for a much less predictable career as a public speaker. She was also about to make a momentous life shift: she was pregnant.

Liz's own mother had been forty-three when Liz was born; she died when Liz was twenty-three. For years, Liz had steered clear of marriage and motherhood. She tells the story—funny, years later, but not at the time—of her first Thanksgiving with in-laws, too sick and tired to eat a dinner cooked to fill and impress; too sick to even eat chocolate pie. The truth outed in a little vial the following day, as Liz writes in *Forty Reasons Why Life is More Fun after the Big 4-0*: "Bill and I watched as the little vial changed color, and the truth changed our lives forever. It was neither romantic nor touching, but it *is* what I said: 'It's a go, Higgs!'

"We were, indeed, with child."

Liz was thirty-three when their first child, a son, was born in 1987. Since she left radio, she's given more than 1,400 presentations to audiences in fifty states and in Canada, Scotland, Ecuador, and Germany. In 1995, she was named to the Speaker Hall of Fame, a distinction among speaking professionals that only thirty-five women worldwide enjoy. She thrives on an activity—public speaking—that many people find worse than death. "If it is, in fact, a joy for you, you've got to consider that a calling," she says with confidence. "In school, I loved speech class. I love the platform."

Public speaking takes a toll on family life, however, since it requires travel on a regular basis to wherever the next engagement happens to be. Liz and Bill had a daughter in 1989, and Liz began writing books in 1993. One day in late 1994, when she was home long enough for him to get her attention, Bill stopped his wife. It was time for their ships to stop passing in the late night. Joining forces professionally would give them more time together, they figured and, in 1995, husband became the director of operations for Liz's business. He's the scheduler, information-systems guy, product handler—and the one who gets to say, "No, sorry, she can't come."

Liz says she works for her husband. She believes the part in Paul's epistle that says wives are to honor their husbands; she also likes to point out that the rest of this famous section of Paul's Letter to the Ephesians underscores that husbands have a comparable obligation: to love and care for their wives as they would themselves.

These days Liz is on her third career: she is now a writer who speaks, rather than a speaker who writes. Once again, she's following God's leading, she believes, as she sits solitary at her work in her office at Laughing Heart Farm.

"In my other two careers [radio and speaking], much depended on what was happening around me," Liz explains. "But in writing, it is always just you and your computer, surrendered to God's call."

One of Liz's books allowed her to revisit, literally, some personal history. Liz grew up in small-town Lititz, in the heart of old-country Pennsylvania. She set her second novel, *Bookends*, an inspirational romance, in her childhood hometown, as a way of going back home and offering it her adult appreciation. "I knew all the kids in my grade for all twelve years. Plus we went to the same churches—in Lititz, you were either Moravian or Lutheran, and I was Moravian—and we played together all summer," she says. "Norman Rockwell and then some."

Indianapolis, where I've caught up with Liz at one of her weekend speaking engagements, has its Rockwell's-America aspects, too. This heartland town is home to good basketball, lots of insurance companies, not-so-tall skyscrapers, and churches tucked in everywhere. First Church of the Nazarene is discreetly set into a newer residential neighborhood on the city's east side.

Liz is signing books in the church lobby after her laughter-as-aerobic-exercise presentation. She is a big woman—her first book was called *One Size Fits All and Other Fables*—and a loose-fitting black dress flatters her tall, ample figure. Her reddish hair and tiger-striped scarf offer a subtle warning: EXPECT LOUD. Her laugh is a big cackle.

Liz is warm and attentive to autograph seekers politely lined up at a table displaying her books. She asks names, engages in conversation, tries to get a sense of the people she's meeting. "Meeting people really makes a difference when I'm writing," she says. "I remember who I'm writing for."

More than a million copies of her books, including five books for children honored in the evangelical publishing market, are in print, giving her many readers—and she hears from lots of them. Her *Bad Girls* books have brought mail from ex-bad girls and girls who are still bad. Liz, who is forty-six, also hears from younger women with histories less littered with all manner of experience. One recent e-mail from a young woman touched her. "She read my first book," says Liz, recalling that her first book, *One Size Fits All and Other Fables*, contained apologies for its flaws, "and she said it changed her life."

Liz doesn't say this to score a point; she says this to make the point that her writing matters partly because it matters to her readers. "God blessed me with writing opportunities," she says. God blessed her, too, with a sense of humor and a gift for speaking. With her performer's polish and one-liner ability, Liz makes faith sound easy and fun. Fun—sure. Easy? It depends on how much you remember about the long ride down the hard road.

Some of the people in Indianapolis have driven a great distance, from other areas of the Hoosier State and from out of state, to see Liz, since this is a district conference slated to continue the next day with a session for women only. "I thought she was hilarious," says Cheryl Yeager, head of a women's ministry group that traveled from North Vernon, Indiana, especially for the event. "What can she find funny for tomorrow?"

Jeri Rogers drove from Pekin, Illinois. "I told my husband, 'I'm going, I don't care what you say,'" explains Jeri, a fan who keeps up with Liz on her Web site and has heard her speak before. "She came out and said, 'I'm a big beautiful woman,'—

and I loved her," Jeri, herself a large woman dressed in unquiet purple, adds: "I love her, I do love to laugh, and she is so good."

Liz's size—a classic woman's issue—is something she struggled with through much of her life, yo-yoing through diets and weight gain on the rebound. "I was so worried about my flesh, I was not taking care of the spiritual side," she says in reflecting on the tyranny of body image for so many women. "We have a new body to look forward to, and boy, am I looking forward to it." The topic resonates with her audience. Her book *One Size Fits All and Other Fables* is in its tenth printing.

New books are lining up on the runway at Laughing Heart Farm. Liz was at work on her third novel, *Every Wind of Heaven*, a historical fiction set in Scotland, when the wind of another inspiration seized her, and she put aside that book to follow the Lord's prompting. The sleeve-tugging resulted in *Mad Mary: A Bad Girl from Magdala, Transformed by Grace*, a book about Mary Magdalene, the first disciple to see the risen Jesus. "Mary's story needed to be told," is how Liz explains the shift. The Scottish novel will eventually be finished, and available in print early 2002.

Liz describes herself as "an encourager." She likes that calling so much, she had it trademarked as part of her professional identity: Liz Curtis Higgs, an encourager®. In *Mirror, Mirror on the Wall, Have I Got News for You!* she writes about her early attempts to describe her specialty as a public speaker: "One time I blurted out, 'Well, I encourage people,' and a woman said, 'I get it. You're an encourager.' Bong! . . . In some [Bible] translations, encouragement shows up as a spiritual gift, right up there with preaching and teaching. Furthermore, the word courage is also [from] the French word for *heart*."

Liz's encouragement cup runneth over. She knows that this, too, rings a bell with her readers and audiences. It makes friends, too. If she has faith in God, she also has faith in her friends. Her literary agent, Sara Fortenberry, also her friend, readily supplies evidence on this score. "Liz is one of the reasons I'm here today," Fortenberry says quite readily. The two met ten years ago when Fortenberry worked at Thomas Nelson, one of Liz's publishers. Five years ago, Fortenberry started her literary agency with encouragement from Liz.

"Her advice along the way about building the business and how it would grow was just a huge help to me," Fortenberry avers. "Any time someone has confidence in you, you have confidence in yourself."

And Liz keeps the friends she makes. "No matter how famous she gets—and she's gotten really big in the world—Liz is still Liz," says her "foster mom," Doc Foster, who helped Liz get ready for her wedding. "I pick up exactly where I left off the last time. She never forgets." Doc continues, "I knew she had done an awful lot. It taught me God can forgive an awful lot. [Liz] is a walking example of what God can do in a person's life."

# Postcard

*Indianapolis*

Double Happiness.

In my car after a four-hour drive to the heart of Hoosierville, I am shoveling in a Chinese dinner of vegetable fried rice from Double Happiness. Chinese restaurant aroma fills the car.

Like so much else that has been assimilated, Chinese take-out feels downright fast-food American here in Indianapolis, a heartland spot. Getting here is direct but lengthy, an escape from the tentacles of metropolitan Chicago through a country-side neatly divvied into rectangular farm fields. Rows of scrubby trees mark fence lines and in between the lines, Indiana crops grow as tall and happy as basketball talent.

Indianapolis, my destination, is an urban setting, but it's small potatoes compared to polyethnic and sprawling Chicago.

Even the construction congestion in downtown Indianapolis on a Friday night along I-65 is fairly civil.

I'm in the parking lot of the First Church of the Nazarene, a typical contemporary Protestant church tucked neatly into a surrounding residential area that is aged enough to boast mature trees. The church blends in here, lower in profile like the ranch homes around it, not especially architecturally aspiring or inspired, but a good neighbor that doesn't call attention to itself.

It's getting dark and cars are beginning to fill the lot, so I go in to get my bearings and find Liz Curtis Higgs, the comedian and author I'm meeting. The church has a spacious lobby, signaling that what goes on outside the sanctuary—relationship-building among people—has importance that complements what goes on inside the sanctuary, where worshipers cultivate a relationship with God.

The large sitting area outside the church sanctuary is practically hotel-like, accommodating both movement and socializing. Like an archipelago, chairs are set in clusters for small groups to chat, and chandeliers shed light on little knots of people conversing. Muted-pink floral patterns on neutral green carpeting give a touch of style to the décor, like light blush on a woman's cheekbones.

At First Church of the Nazarene, the women have old-fashioned names like Leona and Lois, instead of Brandi and Brittany. What you bring to church dinners (salad, casserole, or dessert) depends on the first letter of your last name. Theological expectations seem clear and orderly, too. A statement of faith in a brochure about church membership lists the belief that the "finally impenitent" are eternally lost. No ambiguity there. It doesn't say you can't change your mind before then, though.

My first-generation Polish American mother would have wanted this kind of Main Street, U.S.A., for me (although the church should have been Catholic); my husband, or I, would have been a pharmacist. What a clean job, my mother often said pointedly. Lots of other people think so, too: pharmacists today command a great deal of public trust and respect, much more so than journalists. Ambiguity has no place in pharmacy; it's dangerous. Journalists, on the other hand, are always looking for one more point of view, one more possibility.

# 1976

I remember another time that I took a road into Indiana. On September 8, 1976, I found myself stranded in Michigan City, Indiana, with a backpack, a sinking heart, and no means of transportation to the vacation town in Michigan where I was headed. I was going alone via the electric commuter railroad line to a lakeside spot where I had once lost a weekend with a married doctor with whom I had a brief affair. The doctor had dumped me, and now the train, too, had proved unreliable. Train service had been changed only the week before and no longer stopped in the town where I was headed.

I walked droopily down side streets in Michigan City, hoping for a miracle or a bus. At some point, I struck up a conversation with an easygoing stranger working on a car in his driveway. When he offered a ride to the Michigan town where I was bound, I gratefully accepted, not anticipating anything more than a free ride.

When my easygoing driver drove past the exit sign for the town, my stomach felt funny.

I want some money, he told me, no longer easygoing. He also wanted a sexual favor, he said, in return for the favor he was doing me. He threatened to drive down a country road; he threatened to dump me in an alley. He was driving.

I complied.

Stop, please, stop, please, I begged. "Do not hide your face from your servant, / for I am in distress—make haste to answer me" (Psalm 69:17).

The man pulled his car to the side of the road and let me out. I stumbled into a game arcade in a small town in Michigan. Someone was standing there. Help, I called. Help.

I spent the rest of the long day with police, telling this story several times, finally identifying my driver in a lineup, eventually writing it down so I would remember it for prosecution and trial. The police knew my man, too. They said he had pulled this trick a number of times and they were hoping to build a case that would stick.

It didn't. Months later, in resolution, my assailant pled guilty to a misdemeanor charge of larceny. The far more serious charge of criminal sexual assault was dropped, plea-bargained out of existence but singed in memory.

It ripples back to me now that I am in Indiana again. I'm writing about change. Has my assailant changed since 1976? I have. In 1976, I was Tennessee Williams's character Blanche DuBois: emotionally fragile, dependent on the kindness of strangers. Now, I have a car and a road map of the way.

What is the road map? I think the people in the church I have visited would say it is the Bible. In 1976, I would have found that a pat answer. Reopening the book years later, though, I find it filled with stories of hardship and suffering, a book about those who are tested, for those who are tested, for those who have learned hard lessons that cannot be found in any other book. Even if we have road maps, we can still get lost. This, too, happens; then some of us simply arrive later, apologetic, contrite, relieved to be welcomed by the patient host who has been awaiting us.

Liz is concerned that I will be on the road late at night, and she graciously makes time to talk with me so I can head back to Chicago at a time when I'll still be alert and the interstate highway won't hold only hard-core night owls. I am back in my car sometime after 9:00 p.m. Outside of the Indianapolis metropolitan area, traffic, indeed, thins out and much of what is left are huge rigs—truckers making time, rumbling down the road, and lit up like Christmas trees in the enclosing dark.

The truck in front of me has one of those friendly messages about safe driving. I tail behind it like a little duck that has imprinted a mother image and follows the leader. I follow it for miles and miles, feeling invisible, as though wrapped in a tailwind. I decide the truck must know this as I hurry at times to catch up with it. When I finally lose it after a burst of traffic, I simply find another mother image and settle in behind that one, speeding out of Indiana's blanket of darkness until I am within the halo of Chicago's nighttime city lights.

Two trucks have led me along the way home: double happiness.

# PART IV

# *Remembrance*

# Tracey Helton
*An anointing*

*And a woman in the city, who was a
sinner, having learned that he was
eating in the Pharisee's house, brought an
alabaster jar of ointment. She stood behind
him at his feet, weeping, and began to
bathe his feet with her tears and to dry
them with her hair. Then she continued
kissing his feet and anointing them with
the ointment.*

—Luke 7:37–38

Tracey Helton's eyes are the mirror of her soul.

They are makeup-ad beautiful, the irises pale, you-ought-to-be-in-movies blue, fringed by dark, long lashes.

Tracey was, indeed, in the movies, when she was a heroin addict and prostitute on the streets of San Francisco. She was one of five young adults featured in a documentary, "Black Tar Heroin: The Dark End of the Street." The powerful and unglamorous film by Berkeley independent filmmaker Steven Okazaki followed the wanderings of drug addicts living and shooting up on the streets.

Back in her addiction days, Tracey's blue eyes looked very different. In the hazed throes of a high, she'd walk down the streets of San Francisco's tough Tenderloin neighborhood—slowly, slowly, those beautiful blue eyes half-closed, sleepwalking away the days and nights of her young life among other homeless drug addicts just like she was.

By the time the film played to a nationwide audience in 1999 on HBO, though, Tracey was clean. She got clean partly through the influence of Norma Hotaling, an unlikely Mother Teresa to the prostitute junkies of San Francisco.

Norma, a former prostitute and IV drug addict, kicked all her own habits and, in 1995, began SAGE (Standing Against Global Exploitation), an organization that reaches out to women on the streets. On her rounds of the bottoms of society's barrels, Norma found Tracey—in jail at the time. It was Norma's message that finally got through: *it can be done.*

"Norma had nine years clean," Tracey recalls. "She talked about how I didn't have to live like that. I knew I wanted to go to treatment . . . [but] I thought people must be so deprived."

Nonetheless, Tracey managed to get clean. It took months of treatment, starting February 26, 1998, the "clean date" that she recalls as quickly as one might reel off a birthday. It was her rebirth date. "I had a spiritual awakening," is how she puts it. "I went into this jail and surrendered to my Higher Power. I was at this place where I was tired of struggling, tired of using. I was just through."

"People are not ready to quit," she adds, "until they're ready to quit. I never was willing."

Norma Hotaling agrees. It took her as many as fifteen tries to get clean after twenty years of prostituting and shooting drugs. She quit in jail, what she calls "the poor man's drug treatment program." Both relapse and addiction are a lot more common, and just plain human, than people like to recognize or admit, she argues.

"Don't we all know somebody who has some kind of a problem with addiction, whether food or relationships or spending too much money? Isn't it something we all work on?" Norma asks rhetorically. "Don't we all relapse at some point?"

When Tracey found she was ready and willing to quit, she succeeded in a residential drug treatment program, then got an apartment in the neighborhood where she used to shoot up. She also got a job.

Today, Tracey works for Norma, at SAGE, as a certified domestic violence counselor, a topic she can talk about from experience. As a prostitute, she was raped. A study done by Hotaling and Melissa Farley, Ph.D., in 1995 showed that eighty-two percent of prostitutes reported being physically assaulted; sixty-eight percent had been raped.

At age twenty, Tracey was briefly married—went through a ceremony but never obtained a state marriage license—to a man who abused her physically and verbally. "He was so abusive in the things he would say to me: 'You're fat, you're useless, nobody would want you,'" she recalls. "It took until the past year for me to heal from that relationship." She adds, "I thought I'd never be accepted back into society."

Tracey tells her story in the SAGE office on Mission Street in a building the organization is making into its home, with unmistakable symbolism for the many homeless women SAGE has helped. After exercising an option to buy in late 2000, SAGE staff sent out holiday cards showing them popping out of the windows and doors of their new "home." It will take a three-million-dollar capital campaign to pay for and renovate the 7,600-square-foot, three-story building, a really good deal in San Francisco's pricey real estate market, notes Norma, SAGE's executive director.

Across the street from the organization, like a finger in its eye, is a triple-X-rated theater. The SAGE building's door is secured by a locked iron grate, and visitors ring to be admitted. On one of the doors is a note to one, or some, of San Francisco's prolific graffiti producers, politely asking that the building be spared because cleaning scrawl away takes a bite out of the non-profit organization's budget.

Inside, the SAGE office is a high-ceilinged, fluorescent-lit storefront space divvied into functional sections and cubbies, homey with comfy couches in a sitting area. On the wall are posters to motivate ("Respect is what's sexy," one suggests) and posters to inspire (the words of a speech by Nelson Mandela). There's also an eye-catching then-and-now series of photos, almost exhibit-like, of a number of women on the SAGE staff, including Norma Hotaling. The photos include small police mug shots of the women taken during arrests in their prostitu-tion days. In the mugs, invariably, their lips are set tight, zipped shut. Norma's mouth is especially tight—she was arrested dozens of time for prostitution. The women's eyes stare out from the mug shots displayed along the wall.

The present-day portraits are candid, showing the women looking older, relaxed, smiling, and the lines in their faces offer hard-earned testimony. They are backlit, light cascading gently on each woman. *Life* magazine photographer Jill Peters won an award for these pictures, saying that she wanted to make the women look like angels.

Tracey, thirty, joined the staff of SAGE the year after the photos were taken. She started using marijuana and alcohol when she was fifteen, while attending a Catholic high school in a small town in Ohio. "The girls used to go get drunk," she recalls. She graduated from school with honors and went on to the University of Cincinnati, but by that time, she also had graduated to heavier drugs. She dropped out of college to drift around the country, hooked up in Tennessee with the man who abused her and, eventually—fleeing trouble with acquaintances who were drug addicts—ended up in San Francisco.

"I came out here for vacation and never left," she says. "It was like a bottomless, endless supply [of drugs] here if you have the money."

Tracey was twenty-two at the time—and she figured out a way to get the money she needed to support her habit. "I was introduced into prostitution by another prostitute," she says. The next six years of her life constituted an unending search for a high, turning tricks, being homeless part of the time, and trying to stay alive.

"I was overdosed on speed . . . a guy overdosed me to rape me," she says.

Tracey relates details of her life on the streets without a lot of obvious emotion, without making a lot of eye contact. But she's tap, tap, tapping the edge of her desk in the SAGE office with a cardboard ruler, tapping out some kind of unspoken commentary as she talks about pushing a shopping cart filled with her possessions, sleeping in parking garages, spending hours in the bathroom shooting a mix of powdered cocaine, speed, and heroin into her feet after she ran out of usable veins.

Tracey's memory about events during this period of her life is blurry; sometimes she has flashbacks, sometimes she runs into people who know her or she knows them and she can't remember when or how. She also remembers times when alternatives would occur to her. "God would put things in my way," she says. "Once I was in an alleyway and the stars were out in the sky and I had my shopping cart and I said, 'God, get me out of this.' But I wasn't ready to accept help."

Not everybody is willing to accept help. Not everybody makes it. "Some people don't get clean," she says. "A lot of my peer group . . . half of them are dead; some of them have HIV." A former boyfriend was one of those who died, of a drug overdose.

Maybe Tracey was lucky; maybe she was spared for a reason. She emerged from addiction alive and not irremediably ill, but underweight, wheezing, and scarred with needle marks. She also had one of the common hazards of IV drug use: hepatitis. This, she says, has since vanished.

"When I first got clean," she explains, "I had hepatitis B and C, and my mom prayed, and now I don't have it anymore."

Tracey is now leading an un-chaotic life that includes renewed family ties. After years of phone calls across miles and promises, she sees her parents again, and went on a family reunion vacation with them; she also joined a sister, brother, and sister-in-law for a relaxing fall vacation in Hawaii. Family members met, and liked, her new boyfriend. She's back in college at San Francisco State University studying business administration. She will graduate in 2002 or 2003, depending on how quickly she completes her coursework. Since she's been clean and sober, her GPA has been 3.14 on a 4.0 scale.

Tracey figures she will eventually change her work for some sort of administrative position after she's had more than her fill of the terrible stories that abused and addicted women bring to her. The phone seems to ring a lot at her desk, and she jumps to answer, as if galvanized. She does individual counseling, among other duties.

On the phone, Tracey is listening intently and then responding to a woman, conversation tilting back and forth. "Tell Nancy you want to come into counseling here," she advises the caller.

She hangs up. The caller was reporting progress in her addiction battle: she had gotten into residential treatment, as Tracey did when she began her journey back. "That makes me feel good," she says. "That's payback for a counselor."

Tracey attends Sunday Mass at a Catholic church, but doesn't touch the communion wine. She also attends 12-step meetings, but program rules keep discussion inside meetings, to preserve anonymity. Professionally, though, she is not anonymous. Her story and picture have appeared in local newspapers, and she's appeared on national television several times to talk about issues of substance abuse and women abuse. She gives public presentations as part of her job, a requirement she doesn't mind at all.

"I've had really positive response from people," Tracey admits. Her message is too important not to be shared. "I think I have gifts," she adds.

Tracey's public speaking is one way to make amends to the community. Not surprisingly for someone whose hard experience yielded faith, her own faith is expressed in deeds. Recovering addicts often want to help other addicts, and the best encouragement and most persuasive argument they can offer is their own example that says: *you can do this*. "Giving back to the community is spiritual," she says. "A few years ago I thought it was my God-given right to shoot drugs in front of other people's children."

In other forums, the women of SAGE work hard to discourage the behavior that helps perpetuate the cycle of exploitation and addiction. Tracey has been one of the presenters at "john school," more formally known as the First Offender Prostitution Program, developed by SAGE in conjunction with San Francisco criminal-justice and public-health agencies. Men arrested for the first time for soliciting prostitutes are given the choice of education or prosecution. So once a month, "john school" is convened. Its lessons are about prostitution and what it does to johns and prostitutes. The "students" get the good news from cops and district attorneys: if you make it through class, nothing will go on your record. The bad news: if you get arrested again, it's jail. The "students" also get graphic public health information about sexually transmitted diseases.

And then the johns hear from highly qualified "teachers": the women they bought sex from. Women like Tracey and Norma and others tell the johns about the knives they used to carry around in their purses, the needles they picked up in gutters to shoot drugs before they serviced their clients, the lice they picked off themselves and left in johns' cars, the robberies they perpetrated at the behest of their pimps.

Does "john school" work? SAGE won a $100,000 award in 1998 from the Kennedy School of Government at Harvard University for "innovations in American government." Of three thousand participants, SAGE says, ninety-eight percent have been arrest-free, an astounding rate of correction.

Tracey and other SAGE staff members also do prevention work. Early in the year, Tracey gave a presentation to two hundred teenagers attending an alternative high school. That means that the students already have had some contact with school or law authorities. The students wrote her thank-you notes. "I was shocked when they came," she says, removing a fat brown envelope from a desk drawer and pulling out a stack of letters and cards. There are cards with drawings, notebook papers with raggedy edges, pages with fancy lettering: page after page that student after student wrote or drew to say thank you in their own way. Tracey puts two of the cards on a bookshelf behind her desk. Certification of her training as a domestic-violence counselor is also framed and displayed there.

"The message you gave was touching and encourageable to us," wrote one, "so we don't have to go through those problems you went through. That was a big change you made."

"I'm happy for you," another writes, "because you did the impossible."

Tracey sifts through the pile.

"You're a strong and beautiful person," writes another.

For folks like Norma and Tracey, gratitude is a gospel by which they have come to live. "I routinely just take time to totally stop for a number of days and be grateful," says Norma, who purchased her own home—her very first—at age forty-eight, in December 2000. "We have so many blessings. It does not escape me."

Faith, too, is an essential part of recovery. For addicts coming out of the haze that has hidden traumatic experiences and memories, the hope in things unseen is a still point at which they can pivot from darkness to light. "In order to have a new life, [addicts] have to let go of the past," says Norma. "They have to have faith that what they're doing is going to help them get better, even though they don't see immediate results."

Tracey has one powerful reminder of how far she has come. In her desk drawer is a copy of "Black Tar Heroin," the documentary that captures her at her addictive nadir. She's showing it on a TV in the SAGE office on Mission Street and a couple of staffers are incredulous. "That you?" asks another counselor.

The old Tracey has on a baseball cap turned backwards, baggy jeans, and a flannel shirt—and she looks befuddled and bemused, as if she knows a joke but has forgotten the punch line. She pulls down her jeans on a public street and searches her bruised thigh for a vein in which to shoot her oblivion.

"That's abscesses," says Tracey today about the marks on her leg that the film shows. "That's me in my addiction."

This is how Tracey explains the effects of addiction. "It's almost like time stops in a really bad way," she says. "There's no growth going on in your life. You're changing and deteriorating and you can't see it."

Tracey cites experts who say that drugs stunt a person's emotional growth. Not coincidentally, her current boyfriend is nine years younger than she is, but she feels no age gap and thinks they are well suited to each other.

"I think I've done a lot of growing in the past [two] years," Tracey says reflectively. "I'm learning how to communicate effectively. I pay for my schooling."

Drugs no longer offer something Tracey was missing within. Self-confidence is generated and reinforced by confidence in God. "I have peace of mind," she says. "I don't think about myself in negative ways. I have faith in a Power greater than myself. I think God has really blessed me."

SAGE got a blessing in 2000 when it won another award, this one from the prestigious Peter F. Drucker Foundation, which promotes excellence in nonprofit management. The foundation cited SAGE for innovation in its peer educator program. SAGE staffers (eighteen of the twenty women on staff came from the streets) like Tracey speak to women with whom they share experience—a bond through their bondage to circumstances—in order to give them the possibility of a different future.

Frances Hesselbein, chairman and CEO of the Drucker Foundation, praises SAGE's peer-education program. "Its results show it is making a powerful difference in many lives." SAGE was one of 275 applicants for the award, which confers with it a prize of $25,000.

The winning organization will also have its program showcased in a professionally produced video. One of the "stars" in this video, a story of befores and afters, of hope and help, is Tracey.

# Norma McKeldin
*Seeking mother wit*

> *Moses entered the cloud, and went up on*
> *the mountain. Moses was on the mountain*
> *for forty days and forty nights.*
>
> —Exodus 24:18

Norma McKeldin is standing at my hotel room door in San Francisco and she looks as if she has been to the mountain.

She's been to Mt. Fuji in Japan, and she's wearing the boots and hiking clothes to prove it. She strides in on muscled legs just made for walking on slopes up in the clouds. Her high-tech rain-repellent purple hiking jacket bears an embroidered patch on the sleeve with a stylized representation of Mt. Fuji and the Japanese flag. She's wearing her hiking regalia because she's just come from a photo shoot for local media interested in the Fuji climb.

Norma made the ascent up the 12,000-foot Japanese mountain with almost five hundred other Americans and Japanese to raise money for and awareness of breast cancer in Japan, where thirty thousand women are diagnosed each year and the growth rate of incidence is one of the world's fastest.

Although she went far for fund-raising, Norma's immediate connection to the cause was pretty close: her sister had breast cancer in 1999 and lost both breasts. Norma was thinking about what to do; cutting her hair off in solidarity while her sister underwent chemo wouldn't do much. Then a friend, Andrea Martin, pitched Norma an idea—"something exciting," Norma recalls.

"I said, 'Yes, yes, yes! I'll do it.' And then—oh, God," she says, giving a dramatic mock groan. Martin, founder of the San Francisco-based Breast Cancer Fund, had a mountain up her sleeve. The organization has been arranging fund-raising climbs since 1995, when it tackled Argentina's 23,000-foot Mt. Aconcagua.

"I hate hiking, I hate hiking," Norma insists. "I'm still waiting for the endorphins."

Hate it or no, she shaped up over months, climbing Marin County's comparatively little Mt. Tamalpais with a forty-pound backpack, a great way to burn fat, she adds. She didn't make it all the way to the top of Mt. Fuji, but she did make $10,000 for breast-cancer research. She also made a future.

"Looking at the multitudes coming up the mountain, I knew I was part of a great creation unfolding," Norma says as she describes her experience. "I've created a future for those people that wasn't going to be."

Norma is big on creating futures; the phrase comes up in her conversation a lot. Eighteen years ago, odds were good that her future was not to be; she had breast cancer. Cancer, in fact, came to roost in the family tree. Shortly after Norma returned from her climb, she learned that her mother had been diagnosed with a cancerous breast lump.

"It seems breast cancer has invited itself into our parlor, pouring out tea and passing out lumps," says Norma, with her usual wit. She doesn't think of herself a "survivor" or a "victim."

In the course of her spiritual journey, she worked victimization out of her system, preferring victory to victimhood. Post-cancer and post-Fuji and post-eighteen years of mistakes and opportunities, she is one changed woman—changed right down in her cells and her point of view—from the person she was, working in health-care administration, having an affair with a married man, and feeling very, very angry with God.

"I was cussing and cussing at God," Norma recalls of her illness. "I wanted to drop-kick him so fast it would make his head swim. My doctor told me I needed to adjust my attitude, which pissed me off."

Yet, Norma's attitude changed, little by painful little. Maybe it got burned away. She would come home from radiation treatments smelling of burned flesh.

Eventually Norma had her attitude professionally examined. "I went to a counselor and a psychologist and a minister," she recounts. "One day I was telling someone, there was this little thing, and the only thing I could think to call it was joy—and she said, 'You know, that's your connection with God, even if it's like the size of a pinhead flashlight.' It was always there, even when I was cussing and fussing."

That connection had begun in childhood, even though it hadn't been maintained. Norma recalls making the decision to be friends with God when she was young, growing up in Chattanooga, Tennessee, and feeling gawky, the way kids do. "When I was a little girl I was skinny and had buck teeth and I was pretty ugly," she says. "For peace, I asked God if he would be my friend. I knew I had formed a bond with God."

Years later, the connection was still there, a little dusty but working. The faint flashlight was the light at the end of the tunnel. Norma followed that small piece of light, emerging from the dark night only to notice that things seemed different. It was Norma who was different.

"I remember people telling me I had changed," she says. "How you gonna stay the same after that?"

Things didn't happen all at once, of course. For some, the spiritual path is marked by what Buddhist teacher Jack Kornfield calls "the gateless gates": whatever doors that happen to be there can quietly open to undramatic enlightenment, one door after another. Decision by individual decision, over time, Norma's life changed. She was not the same. Cancer uprooted her innocence, her daily presumption that everything would be okay, nothing would be too painful or difficult. A presumption of invincibility was excised by the surgeon's knife, burned out by radiation.

"My innocence was gone," Norma explains. "The blessing was a closer relationship with God."

That, in turn, affected other relationships. Back then, Norma had been having an affair with the first man who ever told her she was pretty. It wasn't just a seductive and superficial compliment that drew her, however; she liked the woman he saw in her. "He treated me as a person of value. He raved about me being beautiful. I never thought I had anything of value to say."

Still, something about this wasn't right. Some secret presence was working within; Norma was struggling to hear. One day she was talking with a friend. "This light hit my eyes and it looked like a great big diamond on the ground," she recalls. "As I walked over to it, I said, 'That must be a dime shining.' It was one of those little medallions [that said] 'Thou shalt not commit adultery.' It was lying there; it was just lying there.

"I called him," she says, "and I told him not to ever come back again."

After the cancer, Norma's daughter suggested she get another job, since she wasn't happy in health-care administration. She didn't want to be a hairdresser like her daughter, but something else clicked for her: facials. She would do skin care.

It was one of those unmistakable signs, "another angel trumpeting the message," Norma says, drawing out her words. "I got a facial. It was the most profound and relaxing thing I had done; I passed out on the table."

That was a decisive experience. While Norma was training for her new profession, there was a cutback at her place of employment—and she was one of those cut. But the exit door represented a new opening. "God was just moving me to where he wanted me to be," says Norma cheerfully about the seismic shift to becoming an entrepreneur. For almost fifteen years, she has operated Norma Jean's, The Beauty Studio in San Anselmo, a skin-care salon in the Bay Area's posh Marin County. She works on skin and does a lot of listening in her job.

"Instead of therapy, we do Norma," laughs Linda Fetzer, one of Norma's first clients who has kept coming back for more than just skin care for over a dozen years and now makes a two-hour drive south from Hopland, California, to keep a monthly appointment. "She is the A in awesome."

Linda is one of those dream clients: she brings people in through the doors to experience Norma's ministrations. Her nineteen-year-old daughter is now a regular, and even her daughter's boyfriend considers sampling the service. But it's more than just a service for Linda. "It's not just a facial; she takes care of our souls," she affirms.

Linda, forty-three, is happy to enthuse about the ways her connection to Norma has helped her own marriage, given her insight into relating to her former husband, encouraged her to get a new part-time job as an assistant wine buyer after years of staying home to raise her daughter. "We discuss everything, it seems. Norma doesn't just take care of my face," Linda notes, adding that Norma's circle of not-just-clients also reflects back to Norma "stories" and "truths" she can use, sometimes things she may have told her clients when she first met them.

"People are telling her what she taught them," the grateful client says. "She says we take care of her because we tell her different stories. She's incredible with all her past—I think that's why people go to her. She has worked out so very many things, without very much help."

Like Linda Fetzer, Deborah Reynolds was drawn to Norma like a magnet. Ten years ago, Debbie went to Norma's salon at the recommendation of her hairdresser. The two have been friends since—"forever," Debbie calls it. "There was no life before Norma. I met her and it was like going to church."

Debbie even knows the name of this church: the church of what's happening now. At that church, the gospel teaches acceptance and the perfection of the ordinary. "Everything is perfect, and that's the hardest perspective to hold in the midst of challenges and terrible circumstances. There is a perfection in life," Debbie says about what she has learned while lying on the table at Norma's church-studio, talking, listening.

"It's perfectly awful sometimes, but it's still perfect," she adds. I laugh and tell her that her insight reminds me of Vietnamese Buddhist teacher Thich Nhat Hanh, who talks often about the wonder of the present moment. Sure enough, his works are on Debbie's shelf of Buddhist books in her Berkeley home.

While we talk, Debbie, who is forty-six, is stirring a pot of pasta sauce with all kinds of fresh California vegetables. She's been cooking it for three hours, as a treat for her fourteen-year-old son. He might become a client too, she adds.

Debbie says she just finished telling Norma in a conversation earlier in the day about a five-year relationship she recently broke off. The experience had filled Debbie with anger and extravagantly destructive schemes for expressing that anger. "We came up with something else to do," she muses while stirring the sauce.

Norma remembers another decisive stage in the gradual ripening of her faith. She took a course for personal growth, the Landmark Forum, in "1989 or 1990, somewhere in there," she recalls. California-based but worldwide, the Forum is an off-shoot of the "est" seminars—intensive workshops for personal development—pioneered by controversial human-potential figure Werner Erhard. Erhard is not associated with the Forum, although it uses what it calls his "technology" for personal change: intense experience compressed into a short period of time. Some participants, Norma among them, describe the Forum as "a kinder, gentler, est."

Norma remembers her reluctance at the outset. "I'm African American, and this room was filled with all white people," she says. "I sat in the back."

She also remembers how the presenter began. His words were a wedge in the door of her experience. "The first words out of his mouth were, 'In the beginning was the Word.'"

Over the course of a long weekend, Norma listened. When the time came, she was finally ready to speak about some painful memories of childhood abuse involving her alcoholic father, who had died in 1980. "I knew [then] that my daddy loved me and I knew that I could have done the same thing," she recalls. "Nothing separated me from him. We're all human; this is what humanity does. Humanity makes mistakes."

As that recognition deepened and blossomed into acceptance and forgiveness, Norma pursued more ghosts of the past to try to stop them from haunting her. A few years after the Forum, she underwent hypnotherapy and remembers one session in particular for its breakthrough.

"During this session, [the therapist] told me to go find my mother, and I found my mother, and [the therapist] said, step into my mother's life—and the pain that my mother was in repelled me. I *got* the pain my mother was in.

"I regret," the adult daughter adds from the vantage point of years later, "not having more love and compassion for my mother."

Norma remembers one particularly colorful character from her childhood, growing up in Tennessee, when she was around eight years old. He was an alcoholic man who would bend little Norma's ear, the way friendly drunks are wont to do. "He would say, 'You know what's wrong with this generation today? Mother wit—they don't have mother wit.'" Norma emphasizes this homespun word for wisdom as she tells this story. "Mother wit" struck the third-grader as the answer to her problems at home with her father's drinking. Mother wit would fix things. "You know how sometimes God talks to you and he gives someone else the words?" she says. "It's almost like someone trumpeted the words to you."

And so Norma's quest has been for mother wit, through illness and health, through a variety of spiritual systems or techniques that California—where she moved thirty years ago—seems to offer in abundance. Raised a Methodist, she likes and knows the Bible; she also reads and honors the teachings of people like medical intuitive Caroline Myss, who gave Norma ideas about energy and vitality within and how its misuse is related to illness.

Norma just laughs when she's asked to put some sort of religious label on her spiritual beliefs. "I have no idea where I'd fit; a lot of my philosophy wouldn't be sanctioned by organized religion. I'm not a literalist. I look at a story [in the Bible], and I look beyond what people have said the story meant," she continues. "I guess I've been practicing all my life acquiring wisdom. I stopped and thought about the future I'd like to have and I worked from the future to the present. And I do those things that I would like to have. When we hiked Mt. Fuji," she adds, "we created the future that had never been."

Mount Fuji was a school for hiking lessons and spiritual lessons. Nothing under foot was certain; each footfall offered a little guessing game. Would the ground stand still as it was supposed to, or would the earth slide in pebbly bits, upsetting assumptions, making the journey more challenging?

Between the climb and an event beforehand to help finance her journey, Norma raised $10,000. Her effervescence must have loosened a lot of purse strings. I tell her she should be a talk-show host, given her storytelling ability, her verbal quickness, and her confident presence.

She laughs again. She's found yet another aspect of her calling; she can be a fund- and consciousness-raiser about breast cancer. Now she's planning for the second annual "Put Your Booty in the Air and Dance Like You Just Don't Care" fund-raiser. She's talking to someone about hosting a feng shui seminar at her salon. And she's doing a little inspirational speaking, especially within her profession.

Norma says the work of personal transformation is a lot like the skin care she does, which may explain why she never tires of her job. "It really is related to what I do on a day-to-day basis," she says. "I encourage people to keep dead skin off. Nothing penetrates through dead skin. What I do with my life in order to keep in touch with mother wit is to keep removing the dead skin."

"And after my skin has been thus destroyed," says the much tormented Job, "then in my flesh I shall see God" (Job 19:26).

# Postcard

## *San Francisco*

My suitcase is locked and I don't have the key.

Gulp. Poised to settle in, I discover this in my hotel room. Experience may give us lessons, but no way will it hand over a key of any kind. No fiddling with, nudging, or picking this cheap lock, either. After deciding to dial room service to sound an S.O.S (smash our suitcase), I reflect on the sentimental value of the bag—a gift from my parents from long-gone days: "Here's your suitcase, what's your hurry?" Nothing to do but force the lock and open the box.

San Francisco is either North Disneyland or Nineveh, I'm not sure which. It's notoriously expensive. I'm told, too, that drugs are relatively easy to get here. Whether you're buying drugs or real estate, it seems a money pit, with high-priced property and block after block of little places—or glitzy big ones, like Macy's at Union Square—to spend money. The restaurants especially entice me.

In conspicuous contrast to the sirens of materialism by the Bay, but a natural corollary of the cost of living here, is the palpable poverty of homelessness. The weather makes this a mecca for homeless folks. Whether charitably, guiltily, or self-defensively, San Franciscans accommodate this phenomenon. I see large green kiosks that turn out to be self-cleaning public toilets.

After the unexpected bill for a new suitcase—from Macy's, on sale—I decide that my remaining budget will be spent on supporting the homeless. It's hard to see so many disheveled people pushing shopping carts, folks sitting on the sidewalks with dogs, teenagers panhandling, a man with sores on his hands and face. It's hard, too, to give these people money. Another Mother Teresa would stay busy here.

Every homeless person here has called me "Ma'am" and thanked me. If these are the last days, at least people are very polite. I talk to a good-looking teenage boy with his hand out for money. What are you going to do? I ask him maternally. Well, it's just temporary, Ma'am, he says. You don't have to live like this, you know, I say. I tell him I just met someone who had lived on the street for two years and now has a good job and an apartment. Tracey, whom I just met to interview, lived on the streets for a couple years—a couple years ago.

I see the boy again much later in the day, on the same street, near the same spot. Now his eyes are mostly closed—I am starting to recognize the look of someone on the street who has opted for oblivion. Just temporary, Ma'am.

It's all temporary, isn't it? I'm here for three days; with geological luck, San Francisco will be here far longer than that, unless its steep hills slide into the Bay. The steepness of the hills here seems impossible. Walking up Nob Hill, I get more parallel than perpendicular to the ground. It's difficult to remain upright in a city of abundant temptations at steep prices.

I don't realize until later that my first impression of San Francisco is based on a part of the city where the hotel clerk later suggests I might not want to walk. I don't tell him that's the first place I went. But the next time my path takes me in that direction, I do walk a little out of my way so I won't see the same graffitied buildings and fenced vacant lots, with blown trash clinging to the fencing, flapping like a grocery-sack wind sock. So it's not until the third day of my stay—when I've already spent so much money that I'm trying to walk to conserve funds—that I discover beautiful parts of the city. The houses are thin and well kept, rather like the young men and women in their twenties I see on the streets or in the coffee shops of San Francisco—nicely dressed professionals, cell phones in hand. Have communication device, will succeed: the premise of secular self-improvement.

A Pakistani taxi driver who works two jobs to support his family answers questions about Islam as he drives me to the San Francisco Zen Center. I'm taking a break from a religion writers' conference to do a little religion instead of merely talking about it. Inside the Center, I think I am in another country, although perhaps San Francisco is the foreign place and the Zen Temple actually feels like coming home. Lunch is simple, talk does not require note taking, the meditation hall (*zendo*) is simplicity itself: bare walls, bare wood floor, meditation cushions, a statue of the Buddha on an altar-like slab, and deep, empty silence. The *zendo* is empty; the *zendo* is the place to empty out; the *zendo* is full of nothing.

I sit, and the daily buzz of thinking and wanting escapes with a slow hiss from my head, like steam from a pressure cooker, until I am empty of everything except breath, in and out. Whatever I brought to the city is outside on a rack with my shoes and sweater and everything else I don't need to be alive. This is very simple: all I have to do is breathe. It takes no work. Whenever my mind begins to say anything to rush into the vacuum of silence, I look at the little Buddha who says nothing, and my mind grows silent again for a brief eternity.

It's all temporary, isn't it? I have come to San Francisco to ask others how they changed. The answer is simple: change is happening constantly, with each tick of the clock, with each blink of an eye, with each breeze off the Bay. All I have to do is keep breathing in and keep breathing out, emptying. I cannot do one without the other, and I cannot *not* breathe. The work of living becomes simple, however hidden under a pile of memories and obscured by a tall stack of desires and locked suitcase full of stuff. Buddhist teacher Pema Chodron says renunciation is simple: let go of holding on.

Let go, empty out. And out fly memories, memories—and I let them fly, like so many other things no longer of use, blowing around the streets.

## *1979*

I was coasting on therapy, jug Chablis, and cigarettes, when a thirty-year-old friend died of a cerebral hemorrhage in 1979, following a catastrophic illness. She came home in a simple coffin, leaving her two-year-old son motherless. Death was powerful and pitiless; no holding on to life. I flew to Beaumont, Texas, in midsummer, for her funeral. The heat and humidity were so intense that moisture clung to the windows like rain streaming in sheets. I might as well have gone to hell, complete with high water.

My friend's death began to haunt me, so I took the matter to my therapist. During the session in which I spoke about this, he reached across professional distance to touch me consolingly. *You are not alone*, his gesture said.

I began seeing him socially. Then we began an intimate relationship.

And then something was wrong. I started having nightmares again: a sure sign of deep distress. I began having panic attacks. I couldn't breathe. I couldn't sleep. I thought I was dying. I thought I wanted to die.

One night I dreamed that someone was firing a gun at my head. I awoke in terror, sure I was dying. I was alone. At 3:30 a.m., I phoned my therapist-lover for reassurance.

When I next saw him, he gave me a bill for the phone call.

In the grip of anxiety, depression, and fear, I became unable to concentrate. An M.A. in English literature, I lost the ability to read. I would stare at print on a page, but words wouldn't stay together long enough to hold any meaning. Because of this, I could no longer do my job. I was a teacher.

At the same time, I fantasized about writing letters to my students to apologize for my inability to teach them, and I looked for a doctor who could help me go to sleep. I was too afraid to commit suicide, but I wanted to sleep for a long, long time. I wanted to be able to breathe again. And so, at age twenty-six, I checked myself into a psychiatric hospital in Chicago, where I could lay down my head—and the burden of daily living.

I had to call my family. I went to a phone booth in the hospital lobby for privacy. The phone rang; my mother's familiar voice, flat Chicago accent with a little Polish flavoring: "Hallo." I still remember their number. I'm picturing her on the pink wall-telephone in the pink kitchen, pink Formica-topped table, green vinyl-padded chairs that swiveled so we could fidget when supper was something one of us kids thought was icky.

I told her where I was. She began to cry with deep shuddering heaves: "Oh, oh, oh."

"It's not like Dad," I assured her. It wasn't the breakdown the family had learned to anticipate, fear, and wearily respond to as hostility, paranoia, and denial dragged on for weeks, months, entrapping all of us. I tried to explain: "I'm depressed; it's different." In the phone booth, I listened to her wailing. "No, I'm not all right. But I will be. I'm sorry, I'm sorry."

In the hospital, I watched TV, smoked, did group and individual therapy. I talked a lot to my doctor and said little in the groups. "I'm going to stop teaching and write a book," I told her. Nominally an adult, I marked my twenty-seventh birthday in the hospital.

Exhausted by the world I had left and frightened by the one I was entering, I was placed among the functional dysfunctional. We were people who had done our jobs until despair sank pride, penetrated denial, and exposed secrecy, bringing the daily cycle of pretending to a halt. Among my wardmates were a doctor who had become addicted to drugs and tried to kill himself; a criminal lawyer whose wit and bitterness masked his deep sense of personal failure; an agoraphobic housewife who could not venture outside; a depressed teacher who sent me literate notes.

Those of us who could still correctly identify the current president were later moved to a locked unit and mixed in with blank-faced, drugged people on powerful mind-altering medications. These were the "zine" people; the names of the drugs they took ended in zine, like thorazine and stelazine. Some of them talked loudly to themselves. One skeletally anorexic young woman endlessly walked the hall back and forth, trying to outpace a demon of weight only she could see. A sociable man with a bit of an Irish brogue had a hard time getting out any words—his speech was filled with long pauses and stuttering—after he returned from yet another round of electroshock therapy; his mind filled with blanks until his ability to function returned.

While I was hospitalized, my mother came for sessions with my psychiatrist, who wanted to know more about my family. To meet my doctor, my mother spent hours taking several buses across the city, alone. To another hospital, for yet another time, for another ill family member, she came. She did her best.

Once, I overheard a conversation between one of the zine people and his mother. She was berating him as he sat there passively: "You try as much as a dead horse," she told him. He didn't focus on her; his face looked blank.

I left the hospital on a Saturday in May. It was like exiting a dark movie theater after a double-bill matinee. I came out into daylight, and it was spring. Trees near the hospital were blooming.

I had stayed there three months. The bill was $20,000. It might as well have been a million. Insurance paid most; I paid a part of it—I had no job, having resigned for health reasons—and the hospital wrote off another part. I was a charity case.

Twenty years later, I am meditating in a Zen center in San Francisco. That part of my life, too, was just temporary. I wrote a torrent of words in my journal—I floated in a sea of words—but I never said what was wrong. *You hurt me. I'm scared. Please help.*

Twenty years later. In that time I got married, buried my parents, gave birth to my children. I breathe in, out. In 1980, I couldn't breathe. Now I do it without trying. The *zendo* is empty, but I am not alone. My home may not be in this strange city, but I am not homeless. This is all only temporary.

Letting go of holding on is another word for changing. I left my old suitcase in San Francisco.

# PART V

# *Rebirth*

# Debbie Parnham and Loretta Winn

## One at a time

> O God, you are my God, I seek you,
>   my soul thirsts for you;
> my flesh faints for you,
>   as in a dry and weary land where
>     there is no water.

—Psalm 63:1

On the night of December 5, 1992, the "reality" TV show "Cops" is riding along with the Phoenix Police Department. Cameras are rolling when an officer receives a call about a shooting. Police and TV cameras arrive at the scene.

A boy lies crumpled on the sidewalk, one blue-jeaned leg oddly twisted; he is sixteen years old. In compliance with the letter of privacy laws, his face—what is left of it after being shot with a 12-gauge shotgun from maybe as close as four feet—has been obscured.

What hasn't been obscured is the blood. Lots of it. Bright red blood, flowing as freely as water from what had been the boy's face—puddling, growing large on a public sidewalk in Phoenix. A police officer holds the boy's hand. "You'll be all right," he says, and "If you can hear me, squeeze my hand." The officer keeps talking, his talk a lifeline as much as anything else he can do for the gravely wounded boy.

In the officer's hand, the boy's hand lies still, his blood flowing, precious as water in the Arizona desert. In this way, the shooting death of sixteen-year-old Brent Lorentz was recorded on videotape and subsequently aired across the United States.

Eight years later, the videotape is being shown one afternoon to a captive audience. Dressed in jail-uniform loose pants and gray sweatshirts, seventeen teenagers sitting in Durango Detention Center watch Brent, a teenager like themselves, dying on TV. Some of the teenagers swallow hard as the video rolls on.

The person showing the tape and offering commentary is Brent's mother, Debbie Parnham. Debbie also shows the teenage boys pictures of her son taken after the shooting, one relentless, enlarged, clinical view after another. The pictures were taken as Brent held on to life for seven days following the shooting. They show Brent's face, sewn back together with big black stitches. What looks like a rash covers what is supposed to be his chin. The rash-like red dots are the marks of shotgun pellets.

Debbie also display X-rays of her son's head and throat. The X-ray is covered with clear dots—the dots are shotgun pellets. Brent lay for a week in a hospital before he finally died on December 12, 1992. "This is my son Brent," she says as she shows the last photo of her boy's mutilated, pale, puffy face, "in a body bag."

The person whose actions put Brent into the body bag was Gabriel Nieto. Gabriel took a shotgun along when he and two friends went riding around to steal "rims"—hubcaps. Gabriel was nineteen years old at the time.

At his murder trial in 1994, Gabriel was sentenced to 25 ½ years in prison.

"I'm going to do whatever it takes to get this message out," says Brent's mother with emphasis. "Are you going to change the world or are you going to hurt the world?"

Many of the boys in the detention center—all of them some mother's son—have their heads down by now. A few eyes are furtively watering. No one is tapping a toe or bouncing a knee. One boy pulls up the neck of his prison sweatshirt and sinks his face, turtle-like, into the shirt.

Debbie shares the program with another mom, Loretta Winn. Loretta wears a three-inch diameter button with a smiling likeness of her son Ryan, the badge of a proud mom. She has lots of pictures of her boy. Ryan was a three-sport athlete: baseball, football, basketball. The button depicts Ryan in his basketball uniform; he dreamed of playing college ball.

Ryan was a Shadow Mountain High School junior, two months shy of his seventeenth birthday, when he went to a keg party on July 4, 1995. At that party on Independence Day, when the country celebrates all things American, Ryan Winn got in a fistfight. Witnesses say he threw the first punch.

Ryan's opponent, Christopher Columbi, age sixteen, who had been smoking marijuana that night, didn't return the punch.

Instead, he opened fire.

With a gun he brought to an American Independence Day party for high schoolers, Chris shot Ryan. As teenage party-goers watched, Loretta's son died at the scene. When paramedics arrived, they revived the sixteen-year-old shooting victim, whisking him off to the hospital. Twenty minutes later Ryan was dead.

At his trial in 1996, Chris, an honors student in elementary school who became a high school dropout, received an 18½-year sentence.

"[But] I've received a life sentence," says Loretta. "Death is forever."

Loretta was doing her life sentence when she met Debbie. The two look like suburban moms. Loretta is blond; Debbie is dark and petite. Both wear neatly pressed pants, comfy slip-on shoes—the kind of clothes that moms wear when they chauffeur their kids around or help them sell fund-raising candy outside a grocery store. But Debbie and Loretta—who used to be team moms selling candy outside grocery stores—now spend their time in places like the Durango Detention Center, telling the stories of their sons and their families, in "Choices," a program the two women developed themselves. Choices tries to show kids that the things they choose to do have consequences that ripple out over families, friends, society.

"We have been forever ripped apart," Loretta says of her relationship with her son, Ryan, "just because of one person's bad choice. I beg of you," she tells her young listeners, "please make better choices."

In light of their common experience, the two women joined together in 1998 to form Life Sentence, a not-for-profit organization that educates youth, parents, and the public on the effects of violence. They offer their program in jails, schools, churches, wherever they are asked. They spend from two to five days each week in jails and detention centers telling kids that the bad choices they make have consequences that stick around and touch lots of other lives.

This is what some of the lost boys in Durango Detention Center say today. "Thank you," says one. "I want to stop getting high," says another, who has been in the detention center eleven times. "I want to stop picking fights with people," says a third.

How? Loretta and Debbie challenge the boys. What are you going to change in your life? What's the game plan? They've heard it before, heard it from some of the same kids before. They recognize some of the repeaters.

At the end, the boys file out. A few of them say thanks, again.

"You're not coming back, right?" asks Loretta, grabbing one by the shoulder with affectionate sternness. "You should be doing fun things with your lives."

Loretta and Debbie grab a bite to eat from leftover lunches at the Detention Center. They inspect the lunches first, though, joking with each other about not wanting to eat green baloney from Sheriff Joe's kitchen.

This is a local inside joke: Sheriff Joe Arpaio is the jailer in Maricopa County, which takes in fast-growing metropolitan Phoenix—and Joe runs a tough ship. He's proud of his reputation as the country's toughest sheriff, one who doesn't coddle or indulge criminals.

Joe won't let inmates drink coffee or read "adult" magazines. He requires jail inmates to wear pink underwear underneath their bold black-and-white-striped uniforms, uniforms that look like costumes for a '30s movie about a jailbreak. The inmates work on chain gangs in the Arizona desert heat. He installed video cameras that feed live images from the jail to the World Wide Web. Despite political controversies, Sheriff Joe enjoys great popular support, winning reelection to a third term in November 2000.

Sheriff Joe's county jail for adults is right across the street from the detention center for juveniles. It could be the next stop for some of the boys who just heard Loretta and Debbie's Choices program, unless those boys begin making different choices.

Loretta and Debbie had choices of their own to make after their sons were murdered. Both of them were prompted by their faith to do something very difficult. They have forgiven their sons' killers.

During the program, Debbie explains her decision to the boys in the detention center. "It's called the journey of forgiveness," she says. "I made a choice to forgive Gabriel," and she can prove it. Debbie has a picture of herself standing next to Gabriel Nieto, her son's killer. Gabriel stands tall next to petite Debbie. He is wearing an orange prison jumpsuit.

"You can make a choice to forgive and move on," she adds, "or you can stay stuck."

"Once Brent was murdered," Debbie continues, "it drew me closer to the Lord. I don't understand what happened, but it's okay. My first question when this happened was: 'God, what do you want me to do with this?'"

An evangelical Christian, Debbie relies on God a lot. Like the prophet Jonah, she would rather not have been called, given the demands that faith can make. "God is awesome," she says with a smile. "He's my strength, my rock, my everything. I've been a Jonah in my life. It's much better to say 'yes' to the Lord."

Debbie's journey of faith and forgiveness started some time ago. She talks about growing up with a mentally ill father, recounting incidents of abuse from her childhood and the toll it took on her emotionally. She, too, made bad choices, she says, as a way of ignoring or denying her own pain. She got pregnant at age seventeen as a way to get out of her childhood home; she used to get high.

"I was mixed up," she says. "When we're hurt we need to deal with it." As an adult, she dealt with it through therapy, and was psychiatrically hospitalized in 1986.

"I wanted to be healed," she says. "I was willing to work."

After Brent's death, Debbie and her husband, Doug, became active against gangs. They worked on removing graffiti scrawled by gangs encroaching on their neighborhood, and mobilized other residents to help. They also joined and became active in a support group: Parents of Murdered Children. As a representative of the support group, Debbie began speaking at various functions and on radio and television about youth violence. After Debbie met Loretta, she attended the trial of Ryan Winn's killer.

Debbie is amused by her evolution into a compelling public speaker. "It's through God," she says. "I haven't seen myself as a speaker."

Debbie is also a dancer. At the conclusion of the program she and Loretta present, Debbie dances, having developed the routine with the help of a dance instructor. Undulating, crumpling, dashing, arms waving, face contorted, Debbie dances her grief in a "human video," a concept her Phoenix church developed. There in front of the young men, who have mothers of their own, Debbie's writhing body expresses a mother's pain.

Debbie was a Jonah about putting together the "human video." "The Lord spoke to me that he wanted me to do that, but I kept saying, 'I am not doing it, God,'" she recounts. One fortuitous event led to another, however, until the dance instructor told her, "I want you to know that God is going to finish healing you when you complete this song."

Forgiveness was also part of her healing. Initially it seemed at least as improbable as performing a "human video." But as she stared at Gabriel Nieto during his murder trial, Bible passages about forgiveness came to her head, maddeningly unbidden. She argued with God about what appeared to be a suggestion. *You don't understand, Lord. Gabriel killed my son. You gotta be kidding me.* "I feel like God came back with, 'Yes, I do understand. They killed my son as well, '" she says.

Debbie didn't set out wanting to have a relationship with Gabriel. She did, however, want him to know the person whose life his actions cut short. She wanted him to know how her family had been affected. She needed him to hear these things. When it came time to visit Gabriel in jail, she wasn't at all sure how it would go, how she would feel, what he would do.

Debbie let the Lord lead her through the visit, and then it was time to go.

"I went around the table." Gabriel didn't want her to approach.

"I gave him a hug; I'll never forget that hug," she recalls. "That kid didn't want to let go."

Forgiveness, Debbie emphasizes, is for herself. "It frees me," she explains. "I was the one eaten up with anger, bitterness, rage. Forgiveness is a choice," she adds, sounding the theme she tries to teach young people in trouble. "I believe there is a real healing from it."

Loretta is a Catholic who struggled with her faith before it brought her peace. "I never asked 'why,'" she says. "To me, asking 'why' is a waste of time."

Loretta, too, has taken a journey that parallels Debbie's, choosing to forgive her son's killer, who is the exact same age as his victim. "God was telling me to forgive Chris," she says. "I felt led. It was my choice to forgive him."

Loretta sat in the courtroom during Chris's trial, an arm's length away from the boy who had killed her son. She heard bad things being said about her son: Ryan threw the first punch; Chris's parents thought Ryan was to blame because he began the fight. Many of her son's friends attended the trial, and they watched Loretta.

Loretta's faith clarified her choice. "The rubber meets the road now, and I had to do it," she says reflectively of her decision to forgive Chris. "I was gonna stay stuck otherwise."

There's more in Loretta's journey than a single moment of forgiveness. Pieces of her past that shaped her and her choices emerge as she tells more of her own story: a tough childhood as one of twelve kids that she chooses not to dwell on ("It's best to forget some things and for me it's been okay"); difficulties in her twenty-five-plus years of marriage to a man who brought home residues from his service in Vietnam; fights with her kids she regrets in retrospect; a baby lost shortly after birth.

"We thought we had a great game plan," she says of what might have been. "I thought I had it planned all right, but I'm okay with that because God's in charge, not me."

Loretta repeats this several times.

"God's in charge, not me," she says.

In the year 2000, Debbie and Loretta presented their program to more than 6,100 children in schools, churches, and detention centers in the Phoenix area. They were also awarded a contract to work in the juvenile justice system, which would finally give them regular pay for what had been volunteer hours working with jailed youth.

They get letters that let them know they have made an impact.

"I do know you have changed my way of looking at things and for that I thank you," wrote Bryan from Durango Detention Center. "I was gradually heading down the dark path to prison. But you have bumped me back on the track and I'm not just saying that to say it. From now on I am going to do my best and stay away from gangs because no mother should have to go through what Loretta and Debbie, the strongest mothers I've seen yet, went through."

Donald wrote from Southeast facility: "I think when I get out I am going to try and get some help [for drug abuse]. Last time you guys did your program, I went back to my room and cried for a little while. Thank you."

Ann Treis, a Maricopa County juvenile probation officer, has seen group after group of kids respond to these two women. "Something about their program—it's just the push these kids need," she says.

"They do a great job," says Dwayne Evans, a juvenile probation officer at the Durango juvenile detention facility who works with Loretta and Debbie. Evans first heard the two women when they did a presentation at the elementary school where he had been working. "They had a huge impact on our children."

Kathy Donaldson and her husband, retired Judge Paul Donaldson, have been on the board of Life Sentence for more than two years. "We love them," says Kathy of the two women. "You ever hear the saying, 'Something good comes out of something bad'? That is them."

The Donaldsons work with their own nonprofit organization, Arizona Helping Hands, helping high-school-age students finish school and continue to a higher education institution. Paul Donaldson says the work of Life Sentence to steer teens out of the juvenile justice system and back on track fits nicely with their own organization's aims. "Almost every time they go in [to juvenile jail] they are able to sway somebody, or some few, into changing their lives, and this is great because jails . . . simply take somebody who has committed a crime and teach them how to be a better criminal," says the retired judge.

Husband and wife first heard Debbie and Loretta at their church. "They touched us," says Paul Donaldson.

Loretta and Debbie have a surefire trick for engaging the attention of their young audience members in Durango Detention Center.

Debbie pulls out a dollar bill. She's got their eyes on her now.

"Who wants this?" Debbie asks, waving the bill. Hands shoot up. Then she crumples the dollar, tosses it on the floor, steps on it, and grinds it with her shoe.

"Who wants this?" she repeats, picking up the mangled currency. Hands go up again.

"Sometimes our lives are like that: crumpled, torn up, dirty," she says. "The dollar still has value. You have value."

The boys shuffle out at the end of the program, returning to the routine of the juvenile detention center—to their own patterns of behavior, their responses, their thoughts. Maybe the seeds the two mothers have planted will take root in a few. In others, the seed may lie dormant. In still other young hearers, the ground may be stony, fallow, and dry, dry as the Arizona desert just outdoors.

"Our goal is one kid at a time," Loretta says.

Outside Durango Detention Center, a group of adult inmates is visible several hundred feet away. A number of buildings in this criminal-justice complex are surrounded by high chain-link fences, topped with concertina barbed wire, spiky and formidable. The inmates are behind one such fence, but they are clearly visible in their Sheriff-Joe black-and-white striped uniforms that, like a contemporary scarlet letter, scream the wearers' fallen status. The sun is hot, the dry ground anchors palm trees and chlorophyll-green palo verde trees that are suited to the arid land. The sky is late afternoon, bleached-denim blue. Mountains outside of Phoenix hem the horizon, dark in the distance.

Debbie loves to tell stories about her son when he was a little boy. When he was young, Brent used to believe that streets in heaven were paved with gold. She pictures him there now, "digging the gold out of the street and trying to sell it."

Later in the year, during the Christmas holidays, Debbie is surprised by a phone call. Gabriel has called her. "Can you believe that?" she asks. "He made my day."

One day at a time, one soul at a time.

> A voice cries out:
> "In the wilderness prepare the way of the LORD,
>     make straight in the desert
>         a highway for our God" (Isaiah 40:3).

# Patty Henderson
## *The message on the wall*

> *Immediately the fingers of a human hand*
> *appeared and began writing on the plaster*
> *of the wall of the royal palace.*

—Daniel 5:5

The first time Patricia Henderson tried to stop killing herself with alcohol was in 1982.

Her two older sisters, Mary Helen and Sandi Louise, intervened in her intoxicated way of life in San Francisco, where Patty was drinking, and selling and using cocaine. With big-sister concern and frustration, they packed her up and sent her to a treatment center in remote Atchison, Kansas: population 10,000.

Patty was a classic drunk in denial. *Me? I can stop. Anytime.* She hadn't lost a job, a spouse, or a driver's license. The shock of change—going from the high life by the foggy Bay to the sober life amid the wind-ruffled wheat fields of the sunny Heartland—went deep, way down to the cells of her liver. She rebelled.

"I'm there two days," Patty tells the story, "and I sneak out. Middle of winter, with no boots, no coat. I find my way to a highway, hitch a ride, see a gas station. I buy two beers and down them real quick, to stop the shaking. A driver gives me a ride back. I check myself back in. I wanted to get sober," she explains, "but it was pretty scary."

Being drunk makes for some interesting stories, but not for a good or long life. After the drunken freedom of disinhibition comes the hangover of consequences: ill health, humiliating dependence on the illusion of magic in a bottle, and the inability to care about anything except the next drink. But Patty needed more than one dance in detox to change her fatalistic ways.

Now in year seventeen of her sobriety, Patty tells this episode of her life story sitting in the chair of her office in Mesa, Arizona. She is a slightly built woman with graying blond hair tousled in waves around a face carved with the lines of experience. Patty founded, and heads, Women in New Recovery (WINR), a program for women newly clean and sober, that has facilities in five cities in Arizona, Nevada, and New Mexico. Posters on her office wall depict national parks in the West—the forested slopes of Grand Teton, the arid sculpture of rocky Bryce Canyon—where air, water, earth, and sky come together to say: no matter how big, keep it simple.

Patty stumbled into sobriety in the Southwest, a place new to the Kansas City native but a place where it was possible for her to imagine a new life. She didn't get sober in Atchison, but she did manage to come clean. "Alcohol was the medicine that helped me get off cocaine," she explains.

Yet, if at first she didn't succeed, she tried—again and again, going in and out of detox programs and hospitals. "Every time I got out, I drank," says the fifty-four-year-old woman. She passed from the care of one frustrated sister to another, finally ending up in Globe, Arizona, in the desert ninety miles east of Phoenix.

It was February 21, 1983.

"I called my ex-housemother and said, 'I'm drinking again. I'm hopeless and I need to be locked up.' She said, 'Go to Globe.' She'd never been to Globe, but she knew there was a treatment center there. She knew I should get out of familiar territory, where I had labeled myself a loser, a relapse queen.

"She knew I was gonna make it," Patty adds, "when I didn't say 'but.'"

Talk with recovering alcoholics and this stands out: every one of them remembers in tiny detail the exact day the world stopped standing still—the first day of their sober lives.

"I almost died there in detox," Patty says. "I was trying to sleep my way through it." She had surreptitiously swallowed some cold capsules to try to enter detox via the twilight zone of somnolence. Her end run backfired, however, leaving her ill and terrified. She told the night manager of the detox facility that she needed help, and he called a hospital.

Their response stunned Patty.

"They said, 'Don't even bring her.' The night manager said to me, 'Patty, they won't take you,'" she recalls.

Patty was a drunk, maybe dying, and a waste of the hospital's time. Just a drunk, who would go out and do it again and again. After all, she already had. This was the bottom, with literally nowhere else to go.

People in Alcoholics Anonymous and other 12-step recovery groups say you have to hit hell's basement full tilt in order to take the first step. Smashed against the bottom, you give up on your own pathetic plans, acknowledging powerlessness in order to yield to a Higher Power. This painful liberation is called *surrender*. That's what Patty did.

"I really surrendered," she says. Although she hadn't said or heard the names of God or Jesus for years, some things from the Catholicism of her childhood came foggily back. She wasn't praying so much as she was bargaining with God: "Let's make a deal. If I'm alive in the morning, God, I will do whatever you want me to do," was her end of the deal. In fear, she lay herself down to sleep.

The next morning, Patty opened her eyes. The sun had risen as usual, the earth was moving, same as always.

"This is the day that the LORD has made; let us rejoice and be glad in it" (Psalm 118:24).

"That was the beginning of my recovery," she says.

Recovery from alcohol addiction is easier to tell than do, and while it wasn't easy, it eventually became a way of life for Patty, who used that episode as a turning point. She became an avid member of Alcoholics Anonymous, and began living a sober life in nearby Mesa, Arizona. By 1993, having shifted her inner drive from drinking to career achievement, she was working successfully as a paralegal for a large law firm.

Part of her 12-step program reminded her to spread the message to other alcoholics. Rather fortuitously—for people recovering from addictions, providence plays a central role in life—she knew a woman who was interested in opening a recovery home. Patty had earned the financial wherewithal to help, to be the occasion for opportunities that could, literally, save women's lives.

"I say, 'Okay, maybe that's what God wants me to do,'" she recalls. "Maybe he wants me to help financially.'"

But it didn't work out according to human plan. The woman to whom she offered financial support backed out shortly after the house opened, leaving Patty with a building populated by three "hard-core, new-recovery street girls" who needed help—the same kind of help Patty needed when her recovery began. "It was the scariest time in my life," she says. "It was all so very intense."

Patty continued her job as a paralegal for the next nine months, working evenings and weekends at the recovery house. Three residents multiplied into twelve and, for Patty, a new direction began emerging. "By this time I'm in it and this is where my heart is beating," she says. It helped that her boyfriend at the time—a man she later married—was himself overseeing recovery houses for men. "He's busier than hell, he's all happy," she says. "I was jealous of his enthusiasm."

The day she was to make a decision about investing money into a property that was available and appropriate for a group home for recovering women, Patty did something unusual: she got down on her knees and prayed. She was humbly making a serious request to God, whom she had come to rely on in making important decisions. That day she drove a different route to work and remembers what she saw.

"There was a trailer on a lot, with a Nike sign sticking out. 'Just do it,' the sign said. Why was the Nike sign sticking out this way? During the day it haunted me. I knew it was a sign."

"God always talks to me in writing," Patty goes on to explain. "Anything else is too subtle." Patty never found the sign again—she actually went looking for it as a reality check—but she did heed it. Just as her sisters had done for her, she made available, to women willing to take it, a chance for sobriety.

Women in New Recovery started small, as a ten-bed home in Mesa, Arizona, in 1993. The program provides six months of structure as well as housing for the newly sober woman. Residents live in a supportive environment that helps them develop new behaviors and habits that will become the basis of a new and sober way of living. They are required to pay rent, hold jobs, attend Alcoholics Anonymous meetings, and do community service.

A second part of the program, a transitional phase, lasts up to twelve months. During this phase, the reins are loosened on participants as they prepare to reenter the community on their own. Residents graduate to this stage if they maintain continuous employment and sobriety.

For women with children, a third phase of the program, WINR & Kids Family Reunion, reunites women and their young children in a supportive, recovery-oriented setting. Women who want to take part in this program must have completed at least sixty days in the first phase of the program, in intensive recovery.

It's a lot of rules. Patty chuckles as she talks about it and hears her own words—words she would have once rejected. "By the book, follow the rule, 'discipline is freedom'—I've become the person I hated," she says, savoring the irony. "I think I'm supposed to be doing this work."

Although she doesn't do a lot of statistics, according to Patty, she can cite the program's success rate. Of women who complete the program, two out of three stay sober. Some residents have eventually become staff members.

"They make great employees," Patty offers. "Our women end up managers."

WINR is now in five cities in three Southwestern states, serving two hundred women and children. The program budget is $800,000, funded primarily by fees from residents, who are expected to pay their own way, in keeping with the program's philosophy.

"We're self-supporting," Patty says. In mid-2000, she acquired yet another house in Mesa for the program.

"When we get full, we find another house," she says.

Julie Fitzpatrick is a success story. The New Jersey resident has been clean and sober since 1994. She came to Women in New Recovery from the streets of Camden, New Jersey, unwilling to take the next step down degradation road.

"When they wanted me to be a hooker to get a drug or drink, that's when I said 'no,'" recalls Julie about her low point. Rehab often requires a total change of environment; Julie was thirty-five when she entered the Arizona-based WINR.

When Julie first arrived, Patty wouldn't have short-listed her for "most likely to succeed."

"She went through a lot while she was with us," Patty recalls, "and came to us kicking and screaming that she didn't really need to be here."

"I thought it was boot camp. It was the hardest thing," recalls Julie, a mother of three. "At the time I was very angry. But I said, 'I'm stuck here in the desert and I gotta do it right.' I didn't want to live in the streets."

Julie learned so much structure that she still gets up early on Saturday and pays her bills right away, applying budgeting skills she learned through WINR. "I have a credit card, I have a checking account, and I work for the bank. Can you imagine?" she asks with a laugh. "Life is so much easier when I don't have to worry that my gas or electric will be shut off."

Julie maintains sobriety with the help of Alcoholics Anonymous meetings and gratitude. "Patty's given me my whole life back, which is truly amazing, because I don't think I had a chance," she says.

Julie and residents like her also get help from people like Mary Lynne White, a counselor who has been working with Patty Henderson since "forever," Mary Lynne says in one of those drawn-out, deliberate voices that mental-health professionals so frequently have. Actually, the two women met in 1996 and have a lot in common. Mary Lynne kicked her addictions to drugs and alcohol in 1985. She used a 12-step recovery program initially and "since then I've been on my own spiritual journey," says the counselor, who works for PREHAB of Arizona, a nearly thirty-year-old nonprofit agency offering counseling, shelter, substance-abuse rehab, and training.

Based on her personal and professional experience with addictions, Mary Lynne has some hypotheses about who can overcome them and how they can do so. Addicts need to learn two important new behaviors: accepting responsibility and "surrendering." That term, used by 12-steppers, connotes both adaptability and the acknowledgment of other forces that influence outcomes: a Higher Power.

Mary Lynne likes the metaphor of surfing to describe the behavior of always seeking the right balance on the wave of life events. "The waves may come but [recovering addicts] learn how to rise above them, how to ride them like a surfboard. They're also people who learn to accept responsibility. The big theme of alcoholics and addicts is 'It's everybody's fault.'"

Mary Lynne says Patty's behavior is a successful model for clients. "People like Patty will look at discomforting situations and say, 'What was my part in it, so I don't have to [learn] this lesson come again?' Because," the counselor adds, "it will come again."

Mary Lynne's training, work, and life experience convince her deeply that the answers to the question of how to change cannot be learned from a spiritual teacher, clinical therapist, or a role model, although all of those can help. But change sticks when a person learns to trust herself, look inside, and hear beyond inner noise, generated by past pain and bad choices, to inner peace, however small that voice sounds.

"You've got two voices," Mary Lynne says. "You've got your false self, which wants to destroy you, and you've got your true self, which is totally based on love and directly connected with the divine and knows how good and pure you are."

"Which voice," she asks, "are you gonna listen to?"

There are emotional speed bumps all along the recovery road. Women leave the program, preferring the familiarity of alcohol to the strangeness of sobriety. "I used to cringe when people would say this: 'relapse and back steps are part of recovery,'" says Patty evenly. "It's the process of learning that."

Patty's marriage, too, has recently required some attention and repair. But other areas grow, change, multiply. Her teenage daughter has gotten a new dog, bringing the dog quota in the household to three: Magic, a part Chow puppy; Phoebe, a golden retriever; and Max, a "found dog." Managers in the WINR program are having babies: one born, another due. "We're fertile," Patty notes. "Children are very much a part of this program, and we accommodate that as a reality for women."

Also multiplying are the pygmy and Nubian goats that Patty is raising on a little land outside the city. An initial population of three has doubled. One of the women in the program was a "goat lady," who taught Patty about raising the animals.

Patty's bucolic homestead deliberately contrasts with the emotionally charged business she does, working with newly sober women taking halting steps toward a permanent lifestyle change and encountering whatever personal urges or demons led to substance abuse. "When you come off addiction, all your fears and neediness start popping out," she explains. "So I go home and play farmer."

Patty's office is just down the street from the Mesa courthouse, one of the places where referrals—desperate women running out of chances and possibilities—come from. A set of doors in her office leads to a shaded porch overlooking a yard surrounded by a cream-colored adobe fence. The spring warmth is tolerable, the landscape is in seasonal bloom, Southwestern birds trill in desert-hardy trees that shade the little adobe house.

Looking out over the tranquil yard, Patty is talking about her two sisters. It's important to her to clarify something. Her sister Sandi Louise—one of the sisters who helped her—is dead. She died of the effects of alcohol in 1990.

"They saw it in me," she says. "When it was time for me to return the favor, I couldn't. So," she continues, looking out at the sheltering trees tenaciously growing in arid ground, "I help somebody else's sister."

Ask anyone in a 12-step program and they'll tell you what the handwriting on the wall says. It says: *not my will, but Thine.*

# Postcard

*Phoenix*

In the month of March, Phoenix is much greener than I expect. Desert plants in spring bloom are foreign to my eye, although I learn to recognize things common to the area like spiny, red-flowered ocotillo, beautiful to see, beautiful to say. The air smells like citrus around lemon and orange trees, their fruit literally falling off, spilling onto parkways and roadsides. With oranges a dime a dozen, or free, it seems like the Garden of Eden: just take and eat.

The bark of some of the trees is green. These are the rangy palo verde trees, distinctive in their chlorophyll coats. Green is a rare color in an arid environment, a vital outward sign of inner life.

Streetscapes are different, too, with houses seeming to huddle back from streets, behind low adobe walls that confer an air of privacy. In Phoenix, it seems, good fences make good neighbors.

Although the height of desert spring is over, there are left-over blossoms on cacti as we discover on a morning hike into one of the city's many parks. The landscape is lunar to my Northern eye: rocky and largely unadorned except for scrubby low things, some of which are weirdly prickly, like chollo cacti. We take walking sticks, the better to turn over rocks and other things we may encounter along the path. The sticks are useful for ferreting out snakes or hidden scorpions, which bite. It hurts, assures our host, once bitten and now shy of them. It rains briefly one afternoon, causing the cancellation of a hike we had planned into the mountains that snugly rim the city. Everything seems so climate-attuned; the desert in heat is a fact of life that governs the way of life here.

Besides visiting friends and interviewing for the book, I am here to play catch-up with some family history. I haven't seen my aunt and uncle in eleven years. They used to live in hot and damp Florida; now they live in hot and dry metro Phoenix.

I know when I see them in the present, as they approach eighty, I will also see many years standing just behind them, looking right over their shoulders. My aunt, my mother's sister, looks like my mother, and I have been waiting for that picture of her face, with its hint of my mother around the eyes and in the smile. I am waiting for my mother's smile when my aunt sees my two children, both born after Mom died. They are almost as much a surprise for my aunt, who has seen only my daughter as an infant. She and my uncle have stepped in as "grand-aunt" and "grand-uncle" since the children have been born, over miles and time, helping to keep family ties alive.

## *1989*

My daughter was born three weeks after my father died. I had been waiting for a welcoming smile from Dad. The last time I saw him alive was the night of a surprise baby shower, hosted by my sister. Dad was in the hospital, recuperating from what was determined to be a heart attack he had suffered some time earlier. When we visited, he said he was feeling better.

Two days later, I got a call at 6:30 a.m. I lumbered to answer the phone; I was eight months pregnant. The sun was shining that Tuesday morning in the baby's nursery, which was ready and waiting.

My sister had just gotten a call from the hospital. "Get over there, I'll meet you there," she said urgently.

I did not know what I would find. There is a puzzle in physics called Schrödinger's cat. A hypothetical cat lives in a hypothetical box. If a random event occurs, it will kill the cat. The point of this thought experiment in quantum physics is that the cat can be both alive and dead until someone opens the box to find out if the random event has taken place.

I drove and prayed because I did not know what had taken place. For the hour's drive, I could think of my father as alive and believe that whatever had happened was not serious, just some little molecular hiccup somewhere in the great big universe. I thought about the baby kicking in my swollen belly—and I kept praying.

Prayer is answered, although not always in the way we request. When I got to the hospital, my dad was dead. I was too pregnant to be angry or hysterical. But I cried and I worried: Would my baby be born early? I asked the obstetrician. We'll see, he responded.

I had so much wanted to please my father with a grandchild. I felt spurned, abandoned at the wake, standing there woeful, great with child. As is usual when someone dies, we survivors—my brother, my sister, and I—pored over the past, over pictures, over what-ifs. The future was tucked inside my belly, ready and waiting.

One door closed, another opened. Twenty days after we buried my father, my daughter—his first grandchild—was born.

That day of birth was another sunny day, another day on which I did not know what awaited. In the hospital, I walked, I waited, I labored.

A woman in late labor is a mass of stretchy muscle as her baby slowly slithers toward the exit, down an improbably small escape chute. Baby and mom are already trying to cooperate in a duet of movement: I push, you slide. Gravity adds a slow boost. Finally, a baby slips into the world, coated in a bloody wash of fluid and followed afterward by meaty placental tissue. Disposable plastics in the hospital notwithstanding, the whole process is astonishingly organic.

"It's a girl"—they really did make this routine announcement in the birthing room. She had arrived. Up onto my chest this being was hoisted, all fingers and toes in place, beady eyes open, as wrinkled as a shirt unfolded right out of the box; just another ordinary miracle. She eyeballed me almost immediately: "And who are you?"

The next generation was here, and the only way we could get out of this now was to go together. In dozens of photos taken in the weeks that followed, we can often be seen smiling and staring at each other.

Almost eleven years of growing later, my daughter, son, husband, and I—my new family—are in Phoenix, visiting the previous generation: my old family. Just as my daughter—and her younger brother—dragged me unprepared into motherhood, I have dragged both of them into family history to learn, to interpret, to renew ties.

My aunt, uncle, and I are working on some older chapters in the history book: my dad. He could not stand what he experienced in the war, my aunt says. It was too harsh for him. I look at her closely: my aunt's eyes are like my mother's.

He was too sensitive. This rings a familiar bell, recalling what my mother often said to me. It sounded like an accusation at the time. "You're too sensitive," she used to say to me. Now, I hear a question from my mother: "Who are you? I don't understand you."

I understand her better. When I open the door to the attic of the past, it looks different in there. Now that I am a parent learning on the job, I grasp my father's flaws and fallibility. How could I have ever thought the human being doing this job perfectly qualified for it? I stumbled into parenthood, not knowing what I would find, sliding along, adapting slowly to its demands, enjoying mild seasons, and simply weathering the others—acquiring along the way gray hair and an air of tolerance that superficially resembles wisdom.

It is easier to see through that surface when a parent begins declining with age, as my aunt and uncle are doing. Change is apparent: hearing degrades, memory dims, vital organs get tired of faithfully doing their job and start acting out. Unlike my parents, my aunt and uncle have lived to enjoy their retirement.

Must be the climate, I decide. All that fresh, cheap citrus and the Superstition Mountains a constant backdrop, ranged in the distance. Nature's signs: some call it superstition, others call it faith. My aunt says every day is a good day in Phoenix. I shake my head in amazement and amusement: How did an optimist sneak into my family? Must be some recessive gene that flourished when transplanted to Arizona, where the sun shines hard and hot. Organic rhythms here require concession, but repay with fruit for the taking.

Schrödinger's cat is still alive inside its little box. Once I would have looked to check; now I know this by faith.

# PART VI

# Renewal

# Melvin Metelits
## *Repairing*

God knew just what to do to get Melvin Metelits's attention.

He grabbed him by the throat and said, *Shut up, Melvin. Stop talking. Start listening.*

And so Melvin's speech was diminished. When Melvin had cancer of the larynx four and a half years ago, one of his vocal cords was removed.

"I had to learn to live with this voice," he explains. He sounds hoarse, or maybe like he has a bad cold. It sounds painful to produce, but he says it's not.

"My voice," explains Melvin, "was a great part of my persona, a great part of my vanity. I thought nobody could ever have spoken like I spoke. I was a public school teacher. I used my voice to elevate and abase others.

"I'm sorry," he says now, "I ever did that."

Melvin is sixty-seven—"and a half," he adds with a grin that helps him belie his age. With long white hair, grizzled bushy beard, big glasses, and wearing a burgundy beret, he looks like a very nontraditional elder statesman. He shows me a picture of himself in his younger years. Dark-haired and intent, he is standing before a microphone, bent forward and gesturing in a room somewhere. He's talking to a Communist Party gathering. He was a party member and tireless worker virtually all his adult life.

Melvin keeps this picture in a file folder with pictures of his forefathers. Here's his father, grandfather, and great-grandfather—all of them young, dark-haired. His grandfather conveys an early twentieth-century modern image, with his nicely waved hair, but his great-grandfather looks to be from another time and place.

In a grainy old photo taken at the turn of the century, Melvin's great-grandfather, Levi Yitzhak Metelits, is standing before a storefront. Levi was a tailor. He wears his dark hair in traditional Hasidic fashion, with forelocks. He has a long, dark beard and a *gartel*, a belt worn by Hasidic Jews to symbolically separate the upper and lower body and their respective functions. A skullcap tops his head. The picture seems straight from the nineteenth-century old country, but the sign hanging by the storefront startles with its English. The shop is in Brooklyn. Melvin's ancestors came to the United States in 1881, part of the first wave of modern Jewish immigration from Russia. Levi came from Mogilev, Russia; his last name means "snowstorm."

Given him by a cousin, that picture started Melvin on a journey back to the faith of his fathers that he had not only rejected but had actively mocked.

"What was it that made him survive?" Melvin remembers asking as he studied the picture of his great-grandfather, a man unknown to him yet literally responsible for his existence. "His faith must have been linked to his survival."

Melvin had been surviving in a thoroughly secular way. He grew up in Philadelphia; he shows me another picture, this one taken at his bar mitzvah, the coming-of-age rite of passage. The picture captures the family in time and tradition: grandparents, parents, kids. All have done the same things, observed the same rituals, and the succession is supposed to stretch forward generation after generation.

Melvin disrupted the order, however. When he was young, he broke with his family, rejecting them and their religion. His father died at a young age: forty-five. Melvin, then twenty, moved out a short time later. For many years afterward, his mother lived in hope of reconciling. She kept calling Melvin; she hoped one day she'd get the right answer to the question she always asked him.

It was an eternal question: "Was I such a bad mother?" she would ask her son, time and time again.

Melvin answered her thus: "I used to say, 'Yes, yes, you were,'" he recalls, the words slowly drawn out in his precise, rasping voice. "I even used my voice to humiliate my own mother."

In place of family and tradition, Melvin found something else he could embrace so thoroughly it could give him an identity: the Communist Party. The party—its beliefs, its understanding of how the world worked and what the world needed—answered all the questions he had. So he attended meetings, organized, taught, demonstrated—"all of it," he says. He officially joined when he was twenty-eight years old. As an activist member of a small but very ambitious political party, he drew a lot of attention to himself. Who was paying even closer attention, he found out later, were the CIA, the FBI, naval intelligence, and local law enforcement. "When I read those files, I learned things about myself I never knew," he says with a chuckle.

In retrospect, Melvin is almost surprised that his work for social justice selectively omitted one group that has been historically persecuted and marginalized: Jews. "As a Communist, I spent my entire life struggling on the issues of other people and never appreciating the issues of my own group," he says. "But our people have also had a tragic history that I was too willing *not* to recognize."

Melvin made a lot of personal, as well as political, decisions that represented a denial of his Jewishness. He shows me a picture of one of his granddaughters to explain something without words. This smiling young woman is African American. His first two marriages were to African American women. For him, there would be no marriage to the fabled "nice Jewish girl."

The changes Melvin experienced that brought him back to "a people of his very own possession" (Deuteronomy 4:20) came gradually. They came late in life. They began well before the cancer.

Melvin's move away from the party began after a long teachers' strike in 1980–1981 in Philadelphia, when he had differences with decisions made by the party in the wake of the strike. "I started going less to meetings," he says. "Then I started getting other ideas."

Melvin remembers, too, a challenging question from a neighbor who happened to be a woman rabbi. They were talking in the garage of Melvin's coop apartment building in northwest Philadelphia. "She said to me, 'What do you believe in, Melvin?' I couldn't answer her."

Somehow, he found himself taking a course on Jewish identity at the Jewish Renewal Life Center in the area. The Life Center is a program of ALEPH, a worldwide organization that promotes Jewish spirituality, leadership, and identity through a wide variety of programs and affiliations. For Melvin, the course turned out to be more like counseling, as course participants examined tensions they felt in their own Jewish identities.

Melvin remembers one of the exercises, in which the teacher asked him to repeat each set of these words several times, in succession: *I'm a Jew . . . I'm a good Jew . . . I'm a very good Jew.*

"Each time I said it, I smiled more and more," Melvin says. "Then I burst out in uncontrollable giggling. It was like a catharsis. Something opened up in me."

With a blast of pained laughter, the walls of denial came tumbling down. Melvin began to recognize and speak about his rejection of his heritage. "I began to cry, and I said, 'I am so sorry.' At the same time I started reading as much about Jews as I had about black history."

The experience and expression of repentance—checking one's behavior, acknowledging fault, making a correction in course—is a significant part of Jewish spiritual practice, both for individuals and the community together. Rabbi Marcia Prager of P'nai Or, Melvin's congregation, explains the practice with more precision. "It's the spiritual process of realigning one's life with God," she says. She describes the act of *t'shuvah*, which literally means "turning again toward God."

"One's own individual *t'shuvah* is part of one's daily spiritual practice: judging when you're off the mark and setting yourself right," she says. "Communal *t'shuvah* [comes] during the period of the High Holy Days. . . . Yom Kippur [the Day of Atonement] is itself a day of intensive personal and group inner work, of turning again toward God."

So atonement—*at-one-ment*, the goal of reconciliation—became an important part of Melvin's life, as he recognized, admitted, apologized for, and tried to avoid repeating mistakes. As he talks about his past, the words "I'm sorry" crop up frequently. Noticing them, I begin to understand that they are more than just a polite expression.

To avoid making more of the same mistakes, Melvin had to change some behaviors. He readily admits that this required him to trim the sails of his ego and learn to appreciate others more. In short, he had to shut up and listen. "You might say I had a personality remake," is how he articulates it. "Before you have a certain awareness, only your self is holy. You tend to think everything revolves around you, that everything you do or say is of paramount importance. . . . My relationships with people, and in particular [with] my mother, changed. I knew I was part of something bigger, only part of which I was just beginning to understand. People became holy to me."

And so Melvin's people, and all people, became a focus of his energy. He studied and practiced Judaism, coming back to his own beginnings—but seeing them differently, as linked to a great and historic people. What wasn't different was his emphasis on social action or what Jews call *tikkun olam*: repair of the world, another vital part of Jewish practice.

"I stopped being an ideologue, but still felt socialist work is important and good," Melvin explains. It's important to him that I understand that he hasn't abandoned his convictions at all, but he has changed his methods and some assumptions. "I do a lot of the same things I did, and I see God in a lot more things."

Melvin understands his ongoing activism as quintessentially spiritual. "In my spiritual development I've observed God needs all the help he can get," he says. "Our main work here is to help God."

With his socialist affinity and history, he also sees this obligation in light of the famous statement from the Russian revolutionary Lenin about the relationship between theory and practice: "Without revolutionary ideology there can be no revolutionary practice." Lenin also meant the reverse, Melvin, the good socialist teacher, points out. Now he offers this reworking: "Without spirituality, there is no contemplative meaningful action, and without action there is no spirituality. And that," he adds with emphasis, "is a definite critique of those who think they can fly to God and bypass the creation."

Melvin's developing spirituality was fostered and reinforced by the people and activities of the P'nai Or Fellowship, a Jewish renewal congregation in his Philadelphia neighborhood in which he became active. P'nai Or, which means "faces of light," was started by Rabbi Zalman Schachter-Shalomi, one of the founders of Jewish renewal, a contemporary movement of congregations and organizations promoting renewed awareness of Jewish spiritual practices and tradition. Melvin describes Jewish renewal as—paradoxically enough—neo-Hasidism. "We read Hasidic literature, we read and study Kabbalah," he says. Kabbalah is the body of mystical teachings within Judaism. The Hasidic movement today is conservative in expression, but in its eighteenth-century origin, it was popular, mystical, and even revolutionary, seeking to make experience of the sacred—mystical union—available to anyone who studied and prayed, not just to the rabbinical elite.

Melvin teaches Sunday school to adolescents. He leads a course on the Ten Commandments, emphasizing that ethical practice is essential to understanding the theology of the commandments. "My objective is to get young people to realize they can, and must, lead mindful lives." He is also finishing a two-year term as chair of the P'nai Or congregation.

Cancer of the larynx snuck up on Melvin. He went into the hospital four times in a single year: 1996. Doctors first removed what they believed was a polyp. Next they went back to get what they believed was a benign tumor. Then they told him the tumor was not benign. And finally, doctors told him they needed to go back in one more time. Yes, they assured him, he would still be able to talk, but not in the same way. After removing one of his vocal cords, surgeons transplanted tissue to give the remaining cords something against which to vibrate.

Melvin used his new spirituality to weather surgery and recovery. "I began to notice, after the cancer, there were many more faces of God than I ever thought: the surgeon, nurses, friends. Nonetheless," he adds, "I was very pissed at God for a long time."

In the tradition of Jewish patriarchs and prophets who wrestled with or railed at God, Melvin, a knowledgeable debater given his communist background, argued it out with his Lord. "At the services, I would cry and shake my fist," he recalls.

One day, though, he got the point. He let the issue go. He narrates it like this, in his measured fashion: "One day I said, 'My life's not bad.' My sense of taste came back after radiation, people listen to me more—it's funny and true—I listen to other people more. I told my wife, 'I'm not gonna say I'm tired of this voice anymore.' And I never did. I had a new relationship with my voice and myself."

Melvin talks a lot about seeing the holy, honoring the holy. Seen through the lens of faith, the world is suffused with divinity. "Everything is potentially holy: a rock, a criminal, a strange face," Melvin tells me as we are driving through economically hardscrabble north Philadelphia to his home. I note in passing a place that is actually called Hope Plaza. "What becomes holy is an investment you have to make in the other. It's not automatically holy to you."

Melvin serves me a lunch of chicken soup and fresh pineapple in his apartment. The soup is made by his mother-in-law, who doesn't speak many more than three words of English. Her cooking is a universal language, though. The soup is as golden as a curried sun, with hunks of vegetable and meat that retain their shape and character because someone has chopped them carefully. Fresh pineapple in January in snowy Philadelphia is a truly exotic touch, as tropical as all the gaily colored textiles and other New World Hispanic artifacts that are decorative grace notes in the home of Melvin and his Colombian wife, Maria Eugenia Garces.

Melvin shows me some significant things around his apartment, which bears a United-Nations flavor from the cultural variety of collectibles sitting everywhere. Here are Moroccan candlesticks that say in Hebrew "Holy Sabbath;" hanging on the wall is a Muslim prayer cloth; on various shelves are a matzo plate from the 1920s, a hundred-year-old menorah, a strange-looking metal figure of an animal with a six-pointed star surrounding its head. It's the Lion of Judah, made by Ethiopian Jews. Melvin rescues a lot of his Judaica and other items for five or ten bucks at garage sales. There's also plenty of traditional New World-Hispanic crockery and textiles from Melvin's wife.

"She joined our people right before our marriage," Melvin says. (He hates the term "converted;" sounds too much like a light switch, he says.)

Not four days after I meet Melvin, something momentous happens in his life. A son he hasn't been in contact with for eight years telephones to renew their connection. Although Melvin has stepchildren and step-grandchildren, Michael is his only biological son. Michael, who lived for four years in South Africa, tells Melvin he has a grandchild. From the perspective of someone deeply concerned with tradition and continuity over generations, the news is powerful.

"It's completed a real deep gap in my life," says Melvin. Son echoed that feeling to father. "He told me that he missed me."

As chair of the P'nai Or congregation, Melvin talks about some of the congregation's social-justice efforts and programs: participation in an interfaith coalition concerned with welfare rights; support for flood and earthquake relief in Central America; activism by many members in Middle East peace work. P'nai Or also has ties with a black Jewish congregation and a Sufi Muslim congregation, both in Philadelphia.

"Working with Melvin is a delight," says Rabbi Marcia Prager of P'nai Or. Her own background of social activism is comparable to Melvin's. She can't quite remember what year they met, but that's not at all important. "He just walked into my life," she says. "Who wouldn't want to spend as many hours conversing with Melvin as you could? He's so deep and kind and wise."

It was the rabbi who brought Melvin's story to my attention when I first called her. It's a virtual case study of "turning again toward God."

Melvin's mother died in 1997. So Melvin gets the last word: "On my last visit, I knew she was going to ask the eternal question: 'Was I such a bad mother?' And this time I said, 'No, Mom, you were a good mother. You taught me kindness, and I am a happy person.'"

# Frank Plescha
## *The 3Ps*

> *Show me your faith apart from your works, and I by my works will show you my faith.*
>
> —James 2:18

Frank Plescha is a smart businessman who knows he can't resurrect yesterday—so he's doing the next best thing: he recycles everything. He calls it the 3P approach: product, planet, people.

*Product:* Frank's company, Thermal Flux Corporation, recycles industrial tires, the kind used on forklifts and other materials that handle equipment. Started in 1996, Thermal Flux, or TFC, collects these dirty tires with no useful life left in them and reclaims them in a grimy warehouse in north Philadelphia. From the old tires, Frank gets new product: chopped-up rubber bits he calls "Kinder-Turf" that functions as playground mulch. Just call it a nice retirement: from hard-core industry service to a cushy life with kids on the playground. The steel tire rims are also rejuvenated into what Frank calls the "Lazarus" line of products that he's about to start selling. Between hauling away old tires and selling renewed product, TFC came close to seven-digit revenue for 2000.

*Planet:* Thermal Flux reduces landfill content. All these dirty, worn-out tires would otherwise live on for hundreds of years in the slowly decomposing artificial mountain ranges formed by the country's landfills. That's an obvious benefit to the planet. But recycling is happening in another way, too. Thermal Flux is in the heart of de-industrialized north Philadelphia, in a neighborhood that isn't God-forsaken, but is most certainly industry-forsaken. The Stetson hat factory used to be a couple blocks away. Tracks that used to service trains picking up loads of goods and materials from manufacturers still run right down wide American Street, where Thermal Flux is located. Thermal Flux keeps company with vacant lots where factories used to be, shuttered buildings, and some old Philadelphia row houses occupied by the people who didn't follow when the factories and jobs left. Not all the neighbors are friendly, either; the place just got ripped off, prompting some extra door-locking. It's part of the cost of doing business. The whole area is a federally designated empowerment zone, which means it's officially certified as being in desperate economic straits.

The woebegone status of the area is unofficially confirmed by the reactions of Philadelphians who know where I'm headed: "That's dicey," says one. "Let me pick you up," offers another.

There really isn't a lot of point to having a nicely decorated industrial tire-recycling center. Mickey Provience, one of the workers, says he takes a long bath right after he gets home each day. "After the bath they are spotless," he says, holding up his hands, inside industrial work gloves.

*People:* The third recycled P in the company's mission is "people." When I tell him about the book I want to interview him for, Frank says he "recycles" people. He hires guys whose résumés include prison time. He recruits at halfway houses for addicts trying to recover. He's got work for them, which means a regular paycheck. He's also got an incentive up his sleeve, or down the road when the bottom line gets a little fatter than it is now. He will make the people he employs owners if they work out. That's the deal he'll make them.

Frank does all this—honest to God—for God. But the big CEO's name wasn't anywhere in the business plan. "I like doing good by doing well," is how Frank, the company president here on earth, puts it. But the "God stuff" is there between the lines, in the allusions, in the little streams that occasionally run off the main flow of our conversation, which is about tires and enterprise and economic development and profit making and Frank's personal history.

Frank is a retired air force colonel who flew the Phantom F-4 in Vietnam. The tinsel they hung on him for his twenty-two years in the air force includes a Distinguished Flying Cross and the Air Medal with eleven oak-leaf clusters. He flew the Phantom over North Vietnam. Now he says there's a better way, but he also says that guys need to be in uniform because that's a requirement with the world the way it is. "Now I'm trying to be an active peacenik," he says, laying the irony on thick enough to hear.

I can spot another person of Eastern European ancestry, as I am: Frank is beefy and has high cheekbones and smallish, deep-set eyes. Let's back up a little to when he was growing up in Croatia. American planes were bombing his country because it was on the wrong side of World War II. He was driven out of his home during the war, and later came to this country, when he was sixteen—he is now sixty. When he was a young child, America bombed him and his people—and he still remembers "those bad Americans." So after he came to this country, he joined the air force. That way, he would be safe; he would be the one dropping the bombs.

Frank entered the air force in 1965, when the Vietnam War was gearing up. Combat is where he went and that's where he learned a lot and that's where—besides the Bible—a lot of his metaphors come from. "You never go to combat alone," he says. "Even though there's individualism in the fighter world, you never fly alone." The other guys in your formation help cover your "soft side." In military terminology, it's called "check six." Somebody else needs to check your six, and you check someone else's six. Everybody needs to be competent and aware of what everyone else is doing.

"It's built totally on trust," the retired colonel explains. Here is how he saw the goal of combat flying: "First and foremost, you come home. You don't lose your wing man. I lost none," he adds—clearly this is a point of pride. His sons are another point of pride. Following their dad, just as his men did in formation, all three are graduates of the Air Force Academy; all three are active-duty fighter pilots. Their portraits hang on Frank's office wall.

Frank developed some other life strategies from his experience in the skies of Vietnam: he would get shot at, a lot. He took flak. It flew all around him. Flak, he came to conclude, is a fact of life. So he learned to live with flak because he didn't want to die from it. That's still a big part of the way he thinks, here on civilian ground many years later.

"Flak's always happening," he says. "There's all kinds of stuff out there. At that time, I needed to be flexible enough to respond."

So he deals with flak in his fledgling business, which aptly enough is located in the economic equivalent of a bombed-out war zone. Guys don't show up for work; the place gets robbed; a whole shift recently got shut down. Frank has to work to reeducate the materials-handling field about the economic value of recycling and the reliability and quality of a recycled product. After all, most people want new stuff. He uses a chart to teach prospective clients in the material-handling industry about "cradle-to-cradle responsibility"—a better model than cradle-to-grave—for the industrial tires and other wheels they use.

All in all, there's a lot of flak to deal with when you're selling a new idea, running a new business, and using new or at least unconventional ways to operate that business.

"Just before Christmas we got ripped off again," says Frank. "It bothers me if I let it."

Getting ripped off flies in the face of the principle by which Frank operates the place: trust. He learned that in the Air Force, but he's also no fool. People have to earn his trust. "It's a jungle," he says, and this time the comparison seems unconscious. "It's trust within reason."

Right before he mentions getting ripped off, he tells me about a worker who asked for an advance shortly before Christmas. Frank gave him $35 and told him to just take it. A balancing act—Who do you trust?—is going on.

More than once in our conversation, Frank says, "I'm just trying for you to get between my ears." He reiterates his motives. "I see money as a tool. Of course I want to make money, but that's not what drives it. I think if all companies would operate with a social conscience, you could do away with all welfare programs. In order to be really free of it, you have to give it away."

On the asset side of TFC's ledger, Frank has a lot of people to check his sixes. For one, he has the backing and assistance of Capital to People, a multifaceted business tool for businesses that really need assistance to do what they plan to do. It's an investment fund that operates Murex Investments, a for-profit subsidiary that makes venture-capital investments in businesses that meet certain criteria: they operate in economically distressed areas or hire employees with low-income backgrounds. It also requires businesses to pay a living wage of at least $7.90 per hour to workers and to provide them with health insurance.

In a twenty-month period, Capital to People has invested in six businesses, including Frank's TFC. Altogether, Murex has raised $4.3 million in venture funds, and it put almost half a million dollars into Frank's business in the form of a $200,000 loan and a quarter-million-dollar equity investment. The investment agreement gives Murex twenty-four-percent ownership. It also provides ten-percent ownership and profit sharing for the employees, after the business turns profits to share.

Capital to People, which is one program under the auspices of Resources for Human Development, a $72-million nonprofit organization headquartered in Philadelphia, does more than write investment checks. It's also a cooperative business system, which means it supplies help with a variety of management functions and workforce development. "Workforce development" even embraces providing transportation for employees in the form of subsidized van service.

Capital to People runs the books and other back-office functions for its businesses that have annual revenues of less than $2 million. That's where Frank #2 comes in at TFC. When I meet Frank Plescha, he introduces me to Frank J. Viola, Jr. Frank V., as an elementary school teacher might say to distinguish the two Franks, is a business developer with Capital to People. He is there talking business with Frank P. about loans, profitability (when's that gonna happen?), and workforce development. When he's not talking, Frank V. is occasionally scribbling on his little Palm Pilot, even while I take longhand notes with old-fashioned paper and pen. He is most familiar with the operations of Murex, the venture fund invested in TFC.

"I represent a little bit of a different venture fund," he explains. "We're looking to create wealth among the workers." Frank V. reminds me of a seminarian; he's thin, bearded, bespectacled, with pale coloring. But it's a business gospel he's preaching, explaining employee ownership vehicles like "phantom ownership" to offset "tax events."

The guiding idea of the Capital to People program is to bring together—integrate, as they like to say in the business world—capital, management assistance (ranging from shop-floor layout to accounting help), and workforce development: all areas that can sink fledgling businesses or keep small businesses small and struggling. The program is modeled after Mondragon, a successful European cooperative economic system founded by a Catholic priest in the 1940s. Mondragon attempts to put into practice Catholic social doctrine calling for an economic system that balances social justice with individual rights to freedom and property.

And so the ideas of individual fairness and social justice and the traditional religious belief in the inherent dignity of each human being are woven into everything that TFC does, which makes theological discussion less necessary and shorter. Religiosity is cheap, Frank P. notes. Spirituality in practice happens when the rubber hits the shop floor at this industrial tire-recycling center.

"You show me what you do and I'll show you what kind of faith you got," says Frank P., the business owner who's willing to hire ex-offenders. When we get a little more theoretical, he does say this: "Love translates into commitment, and the highest form of action is love."

"Is that in the Bible?" I ask, trying to stir the waters of discussion more.

"Yes, it is," says Frank V. the business developer. He pulls a classic black leather Bible out of his briefcase. "I keep my Bible with me," he says, holding it up. "First Corinthians 13." He cites the apostle Paul's famous letter about the qualities of love. "Love is a positive act."

"We talk about tires," says Frank P. the business owner, "because that's the way it's manifest."

The two Franks evidently enjoy working and talking together. Frank P. the business owner explains it this way: "There's a certain soul relationship that underscores the business relationship."

Soul: there's one of those religion words again.

Israel Rios is the supervisor at TFC. He's a slight, skinny guy with close-cropped hair, a firm handshake, and a slight New Jersey Puerto Rican accent. His work gloves stick out from the hip pocket of his industrial navy-blue work pants. He looks much younger than his forty-three years.

A little before he came to TFC in February 2000, Israel got out of a Pennsylvania prison—after spending six years there for selling drugs. He needed fast money, and he finally got busted, he explains. He was supporting his own cocaine habit as well as the habits of his clients. When he got out, he was sent to TFC. His background fit the work.

Israel, a New Jersey native, describes himself as a jack-of-all-trades with a background in mechanical work. He has done a lot of body and fender work, and worked for a metal-refinery company for a couple years in the 1980s. He recently got in six months of college-level training at nearby Lincoln Technical Institute, but work and school got to be a little much, so he put school on hold. Israel starts his day at 6:30 a.m. or so, and knocks off around 7:00 p.m., since the plant has two shifts. He works Saturdays as well.

Israel is on salary, and he has the responsibility of supervising the crew on the floor. The job is not always easy. "Sometimes I gotta get rid of guys, but I gotta do what I gotta do," he says. "A lotta people aren't responsible."

Israel also works on the machines TFC owns. Several older pieces of equipment used in materials processing are being computerized, and Israel is able to do that as well as machine maintenance. Israel works with Herbie Schwagerl, a sixty-five-year-old retired German guy who goes way back with Frank. Herbie, who just started getting paid by his buddy after four years of helping out around the place—Frank says his friend is not very religious, but he's very faithful—does machine design and Israel puts stuff together.

"I like what I do, like what I'm doing," Israel says. "[Frank] gave me a big responsibility, too."

Although he quit cocaine in prison, Israel had a little trouble staying clean on the outside; he had a relapse—he used drugs again—and got sent to a halfway house for six months, a term that is due to end the day after we talk. He already has his own apartment lined up near the shop, so he can get to work easily.

The relapse woke him up, he says. It reminded him of what it felt like to be high. "Sober," he says, "you feel a lot better. You get more respect."

You give more respect, too. In his selling years, he didn't really give a damn. "I used to sell drugs in front of little kids," he says. "I didn't care."

Israel has his own kids, but they're not young. They grew up with their mother, Israel's ex-wife, in Miami. Israel and his wife had married in Puerto Rico in the late '70s, had one daughter there and a second one in this country after they returned. But the parents split during what Israel calls "the crazy era."

Israel has stayed in touch with his daughters, now both young adults living in Miami. The older one is twenty-three and works in information technology for United Parcel Service; the younger one, twenty-one, is working and going to school. But he hasn't seen them for a number of years. The older one, says Israel, is kind of skeptical about the changes that have taken place in his life. The two young women will have a chance to judge when their father visits them during a week's vacation in the near future.

"It's been a while," Israel says. "I'm looking forward to that."

Sipping a cup of coffee that has cooled in a chilly office right off the shop floor, I ask Israel what he had been expecting about the future as he sat in prison for six years.

"I thought things were gonna be the same," he answers, "but they changed. People change."

Israel introduces me to Mickey Provience. Mickey is a longtime employee here, for three years. Before that he was in jail for ten years for aggravated assault—a "domestic problem" is all he says about the reason for his incarceration. Before that, Mickey worked for years as an art handler at the Philadelphia Museum of Art, the place where movie prizefighter Rocky Balboa ran up the steps. Mickey, who is fifty-four, has worked all his adult life, really, because he had a job in prison working in the laundry.

Mickey moves stuff around the shop—heavy tires he can move by hand because he's a six-and-a-half-foot bear of a guy. He uses a forklift, though, to move large dirty boxes of scrap rubber or metal. As big as he is, he could be taken for a scary guy until he opens his mouth into a great big grin made all the bigger by several missing upper teeth. And he laughs—often.

"I worked all my life," Mickey explains, "and once the realization set in that you got to work, you got to work. I never missed a day, I'm never late."

Mickey lives about twenty blocks away and walks to work. He also attends church nearby, at Berean Presbyterian, a beautiful, dark-stone hulk of a historic church.

"There are times you need prayer in your life," he says. "You need strength to make it through the day."

These days, Mickey and other ex-offenders and recovering addicts are among the wing men and women for a retired air force colonel who sells a Lazarus line of goods made in this factory in gritty north Philadelphia. I think again of Frank's repeated remark: "I'm just trying for you to get between my ears." He says he doesn't think of things like "success rate" among the workers to whom he's given a second chance. "If you go to percentages, I don't look at it that way," he says. "What's one life worth?"

His tall body folded into a forklift, Mickey waves goodbye cheerily as I leave. From far away I can see his big grin.

# Postcard

*Philadelphia*

On a gray winter morning in early January, icy spit is sprinkling from the sky and crusting up my car windshield. "Happy New Year! Love, *Old Man Winter.*" Ugh.

I am driving to O'Hare Airport, no longer the world's largest but still undoubtedly the flyers' choice as the world's most torturously inconvenient airport. I hope I'm on time. I hope the brakes work. I hope drivers don't honk and wave fingers at me on the highway as they speed past. I hope I can see in front of me.

The windshield stays de-iced just enough for me to see, and I spill out of my car in the they-don't-call-it-remote-for-nothing parking lot with a great exhalation of relief that immediately becomes visible in the sixteen-degree air. After the plane is also de-iced, and evidently the pilot can see just enough through the little windshield of his big Boeing 727, I am airborne. We break through the cloud cover and, in thin even colder air high above, the sun is shining and the big star's hot light bounces off the shiny wings of the plane. It looks like it will get better from here—and it does.

## 2001

The sun is shining and it's twenty degrees warmer on the ground in good old Philadelphia, the cradle of American history. That fits, since my purpose in coming here is to gather and revisit history: other people's, mine. I have no place to go for several hours. Feeling like a homeless person, I head for someplace warm and quiet where I can put down the bags of things I own.

The Quaker Information Center is where I expect to find Friends and a place to park my burdensome suitcase and big, heavy, late Christmas present that I wanted to give in person to my niece, that seemed like a good idea at the time. The Info Center is at 15th and Cherry, in the hub of Philadelphia known as Center City, where government, history, tourism, religion, and commerce are crazy-quilted together in a small area best navigated on foot, since many of the streets are old-world narrow.

Friends are important here. Friend William Penn started all this; life here—the good, the bad, and the rest—goes on under the gaze of his thirty-seven-foot statue atop City Hall. His stone figure is like a lofty subliminal message that can be glimpsed again and again from hundreds of vantage points in Central City. Although Quakers are not much for assigning significance to statues, the ex-Catholic part of me likes it that he's perched up there like a guardian angel watching over what he wrought. I'm also reading a book about Quaker women preachers that establishes, through laborious prose and copious footnotes, the visibility and vigor of the role these women played in the religious life of the early eighteenth-century colonies and England, then a single unit with the U.S. still ensconced in its mother's womb. Women just didn't do that sort of thing at the time. Indeed, in some churches and countries even today, 250 years later, they can't speak out.

I'm here, though, to listen. I carefully take note of another good sign in addition to Friend William's shadow. "The essence of Quaker spirituality is right listening," writes Irwin Abrams in an article in a 1987 *Friends Journal*, the publication that serves the branch of Friends with which I am associated. The forebear of *Friends Journal, The Friend,* was started in 1827.

History is a wonderful teacher when we listen to it. Among its lessons: *You are not alone. Who do you think you are? Whatever doesn't kill you makes you stronger. This too shall pass. Old history is theirs who made it; new history is yours for the making.* History is like a roller coaster: it has its ups and downs, all of them of short duration from the perspective of someone not on the roller coaster who can stand still and reflect, or else listen to the screaming, which is what historians are trained to do. All the political, economic, and spiritual turmoil that attended the birth of Quakerdom, the birth of America—the birth of any random baby anywhere—doesn't vanish but just keeps moving and changing. When we turn around to look, what is left behind is memory and historic sites and antique armoires and history books. No people, though; only our ideas of who we thought they were, who we thought we were.

In Philadelphia, I turn around to look at my history in a way I hadn't anticipated. On an *auld-lang-syne* impulse on New Year's Eve, I called up two old friends I hadn't seen in eighteen years, give or take two or three brief visits. My old friends, a gay couple and Philadelphia residents, were (a) alive; (b) very well; (c) together and planning to celebrate their twenty-fifth anniversary this summer with a trip to Europe. Before we lost touch, we had laughed, eaten and drank, worked, and politically commiserated together for five years; I went all the way back to 1972 with one of the two, a college classmate, fellow yellow-dog liberal Democrat and hard-core beer-swillin' buddy.

Something happened, though. Things grew awkward between us—perhaps since my hospitalization in 1980. We increasingly seemed to go separate ways, pursuing our differences rather than enlarging our common interests and experiences. In 1982, they sold the draperies, silver tea service, and claw-footed furniture of their exquisitely detailed Victorian household, donned leather jackets, and moved to New York.

Some things change; some things don't. Almost twenty years later, in 2001, I'm standing in their abundantly appointed kitchen watching Jim run the same heavy-duty Kitchen Aid mixer from years gone by to confect a gingerbread with fresh pears on top. The magazine he's cooking from is different. *Martha Stewart Living* has replaced *Gourmet*. The dog is new; gray-haired part collie Bridget has died and now Fiona, a friendly, silky black, mostly lab, has the run of the place. Jerry still decorates their tree, a ten-footer, maybe, with thousands of white Italian lights and the ornaments hung in little significant sections. Here are the Christopher Radko fruits, there are the firemen, up top a choir of flying angels and, hanging near to them, a glass ornament six-pack of Coca-Cola, the drink that tops Christmas trees and Jerry's "favorite ornaments" list.

Some things change; some things don't. Not all the claw-footed furniture was sold; some pieces remain, refreshed through reupholstery. I do remember the dining-room table and chairs.

We have a lot of catching up, years to cover and things we can remember together that have been separately forgotten. I am amazed at what I remember and how much I have forgotten. This is the time to sort through the contents of the memory box, take out some good old ones and laugh, toss out the ones that haven't aged well, see if anything important is missing, and make a few new ones for the next time.

We talk about that difficult time in 1980, when I was crumbling into psychiatric hospitalization, and they remember what I didn't: "You stayed with us before the hospital, we took you there." I wasn't as alone as I thought—a recognition that has grown in me as my faith has grown more rooted in that awareness.

My past and my memory have a lot of holes. Unmet expectations, unrecognized resentments, unacknowledged hurt, and the erosive drip of disappointment have cratered the landscape. After a while, though, like the lay of the natural land, the lay of the emotional land changes—and what was important becomes unimportant as the rough edges become smooth, the crooked straight, and all flesh sees salvation, somehow.

With every room I walk into in Philadelphia, it seems people have been looking back, looking at the past differently. Rabbi Marcia Prager leads the P'nai Or Fellowship, a community dedicated to Jewish renewal, which seeks to honor the divine spark within and to build a renewed community and planet. She acquaints me with her grandparents as she tells me about the evolution of her faith. We are sitting in a room of her old house in the Mt. Airy neighborhood of Philadelphia, which is filled with big old homes set on softly hilly streets. Marcia has heavy, old-oak armoires in the room; they belonged to her grandparents. A small picture of her *bubbe* and *zayde* sits on a piano, and I know immediately they are the grandparents of her story. They have a great deal to do with her present-day faith. She remembers from their New York house "the smell of prayer." That's an image I inhale, just as I would the smell of home cooking—love made manifest in a pot of hot soup.

Everything old is new again. When we look to the past, we renew acquaintance with it. Time erases what is unimportant, and adds luster to what we choose to hallow, whether it be the faith of our grandparents or the best bad thing that ever happened to us.

I haven't been in my friends' dining room for years. Their house—coincidentally five minutes from Rabbi Marcia's—has filled with an intense celery smell, essence that Jim has wrung from a couple bunches of green stalks and simmered with water to produce transparent soup with a celadon tint. The soup has been clarified with eight egg whites. The home as cathedral—where devotion takes the form of ironing a hundred napkins for your guests—comes from Jim's mother. Those napkins are pretty darn holy, all right.

I've been revisiting and revising history most of the time in Philadelphia, but I have some other obligations, too. I phone home at my kids' bedtime. "Hi, Mom. We're eating ice cream, we got to school all right, we finished our homework, we'll get ready for bed." Their loud, energetic voices float along a telephone connection that links us over nine hundred miles. I can't tuck them in tonight, but I try hard to hug them over the phone and promise to be home for bedtime tomorrow. From the other end I hear the smack of a kiss being sent, and I move the receiver closer to my face to catch it. Tomorrow morning I'll miss out on the humble sacrament of preparing their lunches—spreading the peanut butter, slicing the apples—but I'll be back on the job the following day.

Children make us old and keep us young. They reshuffle genes and write new history with each generation. They bring new eyes to us old folks and to the jobs they will have when they inherit the show and have to run it. As they grow in the meantime, they are little change machines, forever outgrowing last year's shoes and challenging schoolwork. When nurtured rightly and not abused, neglected, or abandoned, they are also deep springs of the unconditional love that is the heart of

God's abundance, the source of all God's gifts. Like a spring, they keep yielding the water of life. They are signs of the ever-present holy.

They are my signs, and how wonderful. God told his people their descendants would be as numerous as the stars in the sky. I only have two, but that's enough. "Therefore the Lord himself will give you a sign. Look, the young woman is with child" (Isaiah 7:14).

What I have is quite enough, including some of the best bad things that ever happened to me. I can turn around and find out I have friends in Philadelphia—friends in the past, I have befriended the past.

Let your life speak, says Quaker founder George Fox. When it does, be sure to listen rightly.

"And be thankful" (Colossians 3:15).

# Acknowledgments

This book is a product of cooperation and generosity.

First, I thank the people who let me into their histories, their homes, their hurts, and their happiness. Their time, candor, and strength make this book a quilt of remarkable experiences. Associates, friends, and relatives who have helped them also helped me by offering their perspectives, and I thank them as well.

A number of people led me to those to whom I spoke or otherwise facilitated my quest or responded to requests. These include Bob Roberts and Judy Rush at Project Return; Jacob Gray at Resources for Human Development; John Lucas at the Memphis Commercial-Appeal; Claudette Silver at the Breast Cancer Fund; Rabbi Marcia Prager of P'nai Or Fellowship.

Having a far-flung circle of friends always helps. I was materially aided in my travels across the country by the hospitality of relatives and friends, old and new. A team of cheerleader-critics praised some parts of the book in its nascence, red-penned others, and offered encouragement: thanks to Mary Caraway, Donnell Collins, Tom Parisi. I thank Jeremy Langford, co-publisher at Sheed & Ward, for asking if I had a book up my sleeve and for support and encouragement as I pulled it out of that sleeve. Faith is hope in things unseen, Jeremy kept saying, and he did not see the manuscript for a long time. As good editors do, he asked lots of tough questions that challenged me to go more deeply. Phyllis Tickle provided prayers and her perspective in a foreword, and managing editor Kass Dotterweich lent a discriminating eye. I am grateful for the professional company of these women.

At home, my children, Margaret and Andrew, accepted lots of frozen pizzas for dinner, occasional absences, frequent preoccupations, and varying degrees of general domestic disruption. My husband, Bill Nelson, is my editor, cook, baby-sitter, and longtime faithful supporter. I am grateful; I am blessed.

# Appendix
## Organizations That Help People Change

A number of people featured in this book founded or work with nonprofit organizations whose missions are to support people in turning their lives around. Giving help is like throwing a boomerang; it benefits people who give it away. All these groups, in turn, depend on being given to. If you would like further information or want to offer support, contact them.

**Coming Clean**
155 Shamrock Industrial Blvd.
Tyrone, GA  30290
678-817-0749
www.comingclean.net

**Capital to People / Resources for Human Development**
4700 Wissahickon Ave., Suite 126
Philadelphia, PA 19144-4248
215-951-0300
www.rhd.org

**The CORE Center**
2020 W. Harrison St.
Chicago, IL 60612
312-572-4500
www.corecenter.org

**Jewish Renewal Life Center**
Rabbi Julie Greenberg
6445 Greene St. Apt. B201
Philadelphia, PA 19119
215-843-4345
www.jewishrenewallifecenter.org

**Life Sentence**
4022 E. Greenway, Suite 11–143
Phoenix, AZ 85032-4760
623-879-8028 or
602-971-3827
www.lifesentence.org

**Prison Action Committee**
661 W. 79th St.
Chicago, IL 60619
773-874-7390

**Project Return**
2703 General DeGaulle Dr.
New Orleans, LA 70114
504-988-1000
www.projectreturn.com

**SAGE**
1275 Mission St.
San Francisco, CA 94103
415-905-5050
www.sageinc.org

**Women in New Recovery (WINR)**
540 W. 1st St.
Mesa, AZ 85201
480-464-5764
www.winr.org